www.wadsworth.com

wadsworth.com is the World Wide Web site for Wadsworth Publishing Company and is your direct source to dozens of online resources.

At *wadsworth.com* you can find out about supplements, demonstration software, and student resources. You can also send e-mail to many of our authors and preview new publications and exciting new technologies.

wadsworth.com
Changing the way the world learns®

LEARNING TO PHILOSOPHIZE

A Primer

Del Kiernan-Lewis

Morehouse College

Wadsworth Publishing Company
I(T)P® An International Thomson Publishing Company

Belmont, CA • Albany, NY • Boston • Cincinnati • Johannesburg
London • Madrid • Melbourne • Mexico City • New York
Pacific Grove, CA • Scottsdale, AZ • Singapore • Tokyo • Toronto

Philosophy Editor: Peter Adams
Assistant Editor: Kerri Abdinoor
Editorial Assistant: Mindy Newfarmer
Marketing Manager: Dave Garrison
Project Editors: Heidi Marschner,
  Michelle Provorny
Print Buyer: Stacey Weinberger

Permissions Editor: Bob Kauser
Copyeditor: Laura Larson
Cover Design: Stanton Design
Signing Representative: Sharon Stevens
Compositor: Scratchgravel Publishing
  Services
Printer: Webcom

For permission to use material from this text, contact us:
  web   www.thomsonrights.com
  fax   1-800-730-2215
  phone   1-800-730-2214

Printed in Canada
    4 5 6 7 8 9 10

Wadsworth Publishing Company
10 Davis Drive
Belmont, CA 94002

International Thomson Editores
Seneca, 53
Colonia Polanco
11560 México D.F. México

International Thomson Publishing
  Europe
Berkshire House
168-173 High Holborn
London, WC1V 7AA, United Kingdom

International Thomson Publishing
  Asia
60 Albert Street #15-01
Albert Complex
Singapore 189969

Nelson ITP, Australia
102 Dodds Street
South Melbourne
Victoria 3205 Australia

International Thomson Publishing
  Japan
Hirakawa-cho Kyowa Building, 3F
2-2-1 Hirakawa-cho, Chiyoda-ku
Tokyo 102, Japan

Nelson Canada
1120 Birchmount Road
Scarborough, Ontario
Canada M1K 5G4

International Thomson Publishing
  Southern Africa
Building 18, Constantia Square
138 Sixteenth Road, P.O. Box 2459
Halfway House, 1685 South Africa

Library of Congress Cataloging-in-Publication Data
Kiernan-Lewis, Del.
  Learning to philosophize : a primer / Del Kiernan-Lewis.
    p. cm.
  ISBN 0-534-50589-9 (pbk. : alk. paper)
  1. Philosophy—Introductions. I. Title.
BD21.K46   1999
101—dc21   98-53732

To Susan

CONTENTS

1 What Is Philosophizing?   3

   Metaphysics and the Nature of Things   5

   Understanding, Evaluation, and Theorizing   7

   The Context of Philosophizing   9

   Are Any Answers Correct?   12

2 The Pervasiveness of Philosophical Views   15

   Philosophy Is Everywhere   19

3 Philosophical Questions   23

4 Assertion, Belief, and Truth   29

   Believing and Intellectual Commitment   31

   Objective Reality   33

   The Definition of Truth   34

   Subjectivism and Conventionalism   36

   Degrees of Belief   40

5 On Concepts   43

   Sufficient and Necessary Conditions   45

   Conceptual Distinctions   51

6 Making Truth Your Aim   57
     Life-Orienting Beliefs   61
     Taking Your Worldview Seriously   62

7 Living Up to Your Own
     Intellectual Standards   67
     Belief Policies   68
     Subjective Rationality   72
     Objective Rationality   74
     Selecting Belief Policies   76

8 Arguments   79
     Deductive Arguments   80
     Reductio Arguments   82
     Inductive Arguments   83
     Using Inductive and Deductive Arguments   85
     Arguments to the Best Explanation   91
     What Makes a Good Explanation?   92

9 The Sources of Belief   97
     Memory   97
     Perception   99
     Introspection   100
     Reason   100
     Testimony   102
     Other Possible Sources   104
     A Final Word   105

10 Flaws and Fallacies   107
     Self-Stultification   108
     The Epistemic Double Standard   112

Contents

Circular Arguments 114

False Generalization and False Dilemma 115

Philosophizing Belief Policies 117

11 Reasons, Judgment, and Trust 119

Having and Giving Reasons 120

Philosophizing and Rational Judgment 122

Understanding Philosophical Disagreements 124

Why Philosophizing Can't Be a Spectator Sport 126

Index 129

PREFACE

This book grew out of my conviction that too many students both begin and finish introductory courses in philosophy with an attitude aptly expressed in the responses "Who cares?" and "What's the point?" There is a widespread view that philosophy and philosophical thinking are as far removed from the concerns of a typical college graduate as are, for example, pondering the origins of Chinese grammar or trying to imagine the mating habits of the checkerspot butterfly. Philosophy is thus conceived as the ultimate armchair luxury of academicians out of touch with the "real world."

My aim in the opening chapters is to show that this appraisal of the philosophical enterprise makes no sense. Once one understands what philosophy is about, it becomes obvious that all of us—and not just contemporary philosophers or the great thinkers of history—have a stake in the answers to philosophical questions.

The remainder of the book is devoted to providing students with the basic conceptual and logical gear required to start philosophizing. The intent is to get students up to speed as well as provide the intellectual context for study and discussion of philosophical issues—inside and outside the classroom.

I am indebted to Robert Audi, Paul Griffiths, David Wilson, Brice Wachterhauser, Charles Taliaferro and John Maraldo for reading the completed manuscript and providing many suggestions. I am especially indebted to Robert Audi for invaluable aid and encouragement. He not only put me in touch with Peter Adams at Wadsworth but also provided many useful comments on two different drafts of the book. I am also indebted to my colleague, Anibal Bueno, for numerous conversations about topics in the book. Thank you to Peter Adams for a very helpful set of reviews from Francis J. Beckwith, Whittier College; Michael Connelly, Longview Community College; Eric Gampel, Cal State Chico; Max Hallman, Merced College; Sterling Harwood, University of Phoenix; Kate Mehuron, Eastern Michigan University; and Louis Pojman, US Military Academy at West Point.

Several philosophers deserve special mention for their influence on what I have written. I am indebted to Paul Helm's book on belief policies and Richard Foley's work on rationality, as I am to all of Robert Audi's work in epistemology. Special acknowledgment is also due to Paul Griffiths, William Wainwright, William Rowe, and David Wilson, whose work and friendship have continually exemplified the pleasure and worth of learning—and continuing—to philosophize.

A final acknowledgment is due to my wife, Susan Kiernan-Lewis. Her love and friendship are the icing on the cake of a philosophical life.

D.K-L.

LEARNING TO PHILOSOPHIZE

A PRIMER

CHAPTER 1

What Is Philosophizing?

IF YOU ARE LIKE MOST STUDENTS TAKING A FIRST COURSE IN PHI-losophy, you're probably a little puzzled about what you've signed up for and what, exactly, you're going to be studying. This makes a "philosophy" course a special case, for you certainly don't have the same sort of puzzlement when you sign up for a course in, say, biology or computer science. You *know* what you're in for, because you have a pretty clear idea of the subject matter—that is, of what biology and computer science are *about*. But what's philosophy about?

I'll return to that question shortly, but first I want to point out to you that philosophy as an academic discipline is not like most of the other disciplines you can major in at a college or university. Let's suppose that by "biologists" and "historians" we mean persons who have had extensive training—a Ph.D. or the equivalent—in their field. Now, in each of these cases, we can cite innumerable statements that are universally accepted by anyone in each field. For example:

- Biologists say that DNA has a lot to do with inheritance, that mammals suckle their young, and that insects were around long before toads.
- Historians say that the Pyramids were built long before the Eiffel Tower, that Germany lost in World War II, and that Confucius was not a Native American.
- Physicists say that the positively charged hydrogen ion is a proton, that nothing travels faster than the speed of light, and that a molecule of uranium is heavier than a carbon molecule.

This is not to say that trained biologists, historians, or physicists agree about *everything*: they don't and probably never will. Rather, virtually everyone in these fields accepts a large body of *noncontroversial information.* There is a long list of biological (or historical or mathematical) questions to which every trained biologist (or historian or mathematician) knows the answer. Knowing the answers is part of what it means to be educated in these fields. Therefore, when you take "Introduction to . . ." courses, you usually get an introduction to what your professors consider noncontroversial information to anyone, such as themselves, with a Ph.D. in the field. In most cases, you will learn the stock of standard noncontroversial answers to standard noncontroversial questions in the field; learning these answers is essentially learning What Biologists (or Historians or Physicists) Say. You will learn what those trained in the field regard as the noncontroversial "findings" of that intellectual enterprise.

Of course, you probably already know all of this, and it's because you do that you're likely to make the mistake of thinking that there must be some long list of statements that begin with the words "Philosophers say. . . ." There must be, you may think, some stock of standard philosophical questions to which all educated philosophers know (or think they know) the correct standard answers and that you will be expected to learn these answers in an introductory course in philosophy.

Well, it isn't so. Philosophy is not like that. First, there just are no *noncontroversial* answers to philosophical questions. (But don't take this wrongly: this doesn't mean there aren't any *correct* answers. More on this at the end of the chapter.) For example, the question "What is philosophy?" is itself a philosophical question to which living and dead philosophers (professional and not) have given different answers. Even the question "What is a philosophical question?" is a philosophical question open to numerous answers.

Metaphysics and the Nature of Things

A good way to begin to get a handle on the nature of philosophical questions is to look at the questions central to an important branch of philosophy, the area known as "metaphysics." You're familiar with the distinction between the way things appear to be (for example, the way the surface of a road looks wet in the distance on a hot summer day) and the way things really are (the road is dry). Metaphysics attempts to get behind the appearances to find out the truth about the ultimate nature of things.

Although they aren't usually very well thought out, most of us either consciously or unconsciously have answers to three "really big" questions that it is the task of metaphysics to answer:

1. What is ultimately real?

Here are some controversial answers:

- "There is just the physical universe studied by the natural sciences."
- "There are only minds and their thoughts."
- "There are immaterial spirits and material objects."

2. Why does whatever is real exist?

   Some answers:

   - "There is no reason why the collection of all real items (which is just the physical universe) exists. It just does."
   - "God exists because his existence is necessary. Everything else exists because God chose to create it."
   - "The physical universe is an illusion generated by Atman, the ultimate transcendent reality. Atman has no cause and causes everything else."

3. What is the place of human beings in the real?

   Some familiar answers:

   - "Human beings are merely complex constituents of the physical universe, accidental products—like frogs, trees, and all terrestrial species—of a mindless, purposeless evolutionary process."
   - "Human beings are a composite of a physical body and preexistent reincarnated soul, which remains trapped in the cycle of death and rebirth unless that soul achieves Nirvana."
   - "Human beings are rational, moral agents who survive the death of their bodies and whose purpose is to love and worship God forever."

Most people don't think these three philosophical questions aren't worth pondering, or can't be answered correctly (or incorrectly), or are just unanswerable. In fact, each of us carries around in our minds a kind of mental map of The Way Things Are that serves to guide us in our thinking, planning, and acting and that, at least in part, provides answers to these three metaphysical questions. Isn't it worthwhile to consider whether your personal mental map is accurate? Isn't that the sort of thing a responsible person who is serious about life would do?

However, to deliberate about the answers to philosophical questions is to engage in philosophical reasoning. As philosophers like to say, it is "to do philosophy." Philosophy is best understood as this activity of philosophizing, and not as any set of widely accepted doctrines and beliefs. Moreover, for this activity to go beyond a frivolous diversion, there must be something to be got right.

Understanding, Evaluation, and Theorizing

The activity of philosophizing may be divided into three central subactivities. First, there is the attempt to *understand* both philosophical questions and the various answers to them. Second, there is the evaluation of reasons. And third, there is higher-level theorizing.

Prior to evaluating the reasons or evidence put forward by someone for their philosophical view, you must make sure that you understand what they are saying. Otherwise, you won't really know what is at issue. That's why philosophers traditionally have spent a lot of time and energy on questions of meaning.

Suppose I ask you whether the following statement is true: "Snafflejabobbles trillapifilate." Unfortunately, you can't answer the question until you understand what the statement means—that is, until you first understand what it is that I am saying (if anything). Now consider the question "Can a computer think?" To answer this question, you have to determine the meaning of our concept or idea of "thinking." Once you've got a general account of what a thinking thing is or can do, you can then use this understanding to answer the question.

Notice that the mention of "understanding" an idea or statement brings with it the idea of *mis*understanding, and thereby the idea of correctness. I cannot know that an answer is correct if it is in fact *in*correct, and I cannot truly be said to understand what I *mis*understand. There will be no hope of answering a question such as "Can a computer think?" unless I correctly understand what I might have misunderstood.

The second central subactivity of philosophizing is the evaluation of reasons. Here the aim is to take a close look at the evidence and arguments in favor of different answers to philosophical questions. Old philosophy textbooks said that philosophy begins in wonder. The world does appear to be a wondrous and puzzling place. That there should be anything at all instead of nothing has seemed an extraordinary fact to many philosophically minded people. Human curiosity seems driven to consider the ultimate nature of things and how human beings fit into the "big picture." If philosophers throughout history have shared any trait in common, it is the tendency to wonder why a particular philosophical claim is, or should be, believed, a wonderment that initiates investigation into and reflection on the reasons offered or offerable in support of that claim.

Note that these two subactivities will often be intertwined and interdependent in practice. The articulation and clarification of a philosophical view will usually involve arguing that some reading of the view is the best and proper way to understand it. And you may decide that there just is no way to understand some view because the view is demonstrably absurd or confused. In that case, the attempt to understand will itself provide you with a reason for rejecting the view.

Philosophizing is not limited to the evaluation of reasons or the elucidation of philosophical ideas and views. Philosophers have historically engaged in higher-level theorizing that involves developing new ways to look at fundamental issues such as freedom, knowledge, and morality. They attempt, for instance, to give an account of human freedom that is plausible and defensible—that will bear up under the critical scrutiny of the serious inquirer into the nature of freedom. Much of this higher-level theorizing is generated by the attempt to answer questions of the form "What is the nature of _____?" For example: What is the nature of causation? What is the nature of persons? What is the nature of knowledge? What is the nature of reference? Imagination and creativity play a key role in this theorizing, which is the third central subactivity of philosophizing.

The Context of Philosophizing

It *never* counts as philosophizing merely to quote Plato's, Descartes's, Nietzsche's, or any other famous thinker's answer to some philosophical question as though that settles the matter. There are no canonical authorities or texts in philosophy. For this reason, philosophizing is not parroting great philosophers. What matters is not whether, say, Descartes said human beings have souls, but whether you think his reasons are good reasons for saying so. Of course, if you are interested in the question of whether human beings have souls, you'll probably want to look at what Descartes and other philosophers in history have said on the topic. But if you are philosophizing, and not merely reading for historical interest, you'll want to think through the arguments of the great philosophers for yourself.

Philosophizing is intrinsically conversational. Our reasons for belief get developed and refined in the course of arguing with others and even with ourselves. This is where reading comes in, because if we want to grapple with a philosophical issue, then we will want to know what others—past and present—have said about the positions we wish to defend or reject.

Philosophizing presupposes a love of reason and a general willingness to subject your beliefs to critical reflection and scrutiny. As this statement suggests, philosophizing most naturally arises against a background of key emotional commitments. If you don't really care about truth or don't fear error, you may not be inclined to scrutinize your beliefs at all. Ideally, you must be willing to value a belief more highly because it is true than because it happens to be your own. If you are merely trying to get me to hold your views, you may not be philosophizing at all but only propagandizing, and I may be justified in disregarding everything you say. (Note, however, that your arguments may still be good arguments even though you are more interested in getting me to endorse their conclusions than in supporting the truth of those conclusions.) Philosophizing is not propagandizing because the aim of propagandizing is at best mere persuasion, not truth. To be taken seriously in a philosophical discussion, you have to be willing to give up your own beliefs, if you decide they are false, in exchange for true ones, and you have to see this not as a bad thing but as a welcome benefit. After all, if what you want is the *correct* answer to a philosophical question, then you can only gain by giving up an incorrect answer.

I don't mean to suggest that most or all of the philosophical beliefs you bring to your initial contact with philosophy are false or confused or irrational, or that a philosophical belief held nonreflectively is therefore likely to be false. I do mean to suggest that there are well-known obstacles to the ideals of philosophizing sketched in the last paragraph. You may be said to care about the answer to a philosophical question in two senses. First, you may want to know the right answer to the question. Second, you may strongly desire that a certain answer to that question be the right one. If you care deeply about the answers to philosophical questions in the first sense, you will be moved (or moveable) by evidence and argument. Those who care deeply about answers to philosophical questions in the second sense will be moved by factors such as political loyalties and antipathies, prejudicial preference for their social group, the desire for emotional comfort, the desire not to appear old-fashioned, the desire to appear progressive or "scientific," and so on. None of us, including (perhaps especially) your professors, are immune to the biases generated by such nonrational factors.

Our preferences, attitudes, biases, likes and dislikes, desires and aversions can create an obstacle to serious reflection. However, it doesn't follow that "People are going to believe whatever they believe anyway." Often evidence and argument lead us to change our beliefs, which wouldn't occur if we didn't have an interest in answers that are *really* right (and not just "right for me"). At any rate, I will be assuming in what follows that evidence and argument do sometimes lead persons to change their beliefs or to retain the beliefs they already have.

Philosophy—that is, philosophizing—is fundamentally interactive. It is like a lively conversation on a controversial subject, not like passively watching television. So it is better to think of philosophy as an activity, not just a set of doctrines. This bears repeating: Philosophy is the activity of grappling with philosophical questions, not any set of doctrines. If we characterize philosophizing in terms of adherence to a specific set of doctrines, we will be talking nonsense when we refer to the "history of philosophy." From the historical point of view, there just is no such thing as the "findings" of philosophy. Consider, for example, the so-called "Western" philosophical tradition. By any plausible standard, the ancient Greek philosophers Plato and Aristotle; the thirteenth-century theologian Thomas Aquinas; the French philosopher and mathematician Descartes; the British philosophers David Hume and Thomas Hobbes; the nineteenth-century German philosophers Karl Marx and Friedrich Nietzsche; and twentieth-century philosophers Bertrand Russell, Ludwig Wittgenstein, Hilary Putnam, and W. V. O. Quine are all important members of this tradition. They are undeniably "Western" philosophers. Yet there is no consensus among them on the answers to such questions as "Is there a God?" "Do human beings have free will?" "Is morality invented or discovered?" and "Can human beings survive the death of their bodies?" It makes no sense to say "I reject Western philosophy" simply because famous Western philosophers, past and present, haven't always agreed on the answers when they've addressed the same questions.

Are Any Answers Correct?

I began this chapter with the idea that there are no non-controversial answers in philosophy. You shouldn't take this to mean that, therefore, "anything goes" when it comes to philosophical stances. Nor should you think that this means there is no point in seeking correct answers to philosophical questions. It is helpful here to distinguish between two ways in which the word *correct* is ordinarily used. First, it is often used to mean "accepted as (or believed to be) correct by those in a position to know." It is in this sense that we might say that Newton's physics, for example, was "correct" according to physicists living in 1800. But in this sense the big bang theory about the history of the physical universe is now correct. Of course, this sense of "correctness" has no necessary connection to the truth—that is, to what is *really* the case. What is "believed to be correct" may turn out—as did Newton's physics—to be incorrect. (Obviously what is believed to be correct also really may be correct.) "*Really* correct"—and not just "believed to be correct"—is the second way we use the word *correct.*

We need this second idea of correctness to make sense of the idea of a mistaken belief. For if *correct* only meant "believed by someone to be correct," there could be no such thing as a mistaken belief. Believing would make it so. For example, suppose you believe Oswald acted alone in killing President Kennedy, although your friend Jennifer believes Oswald was involved in a conspiracy of culprits. If *correct* meant only "believed by someone to be correct," then you could not say that Jennifer has an *in*correct or mistaken view. Stranger still, if *correct* meant only "believed to be correct," once you realize what you believe about Oswald, it would be absurd for you to wonder whether your belief might be incorrect. About the only thing you can say to a person who tells you there are no correct-in-the-second-sense beliefs is that, then, he can't be telling anything really correct (as opposed to something believed by him to be so).

Now consider the philosophical question "Is it possible for a human being to survive his or her own death?" It would seem that there are only two possible answers to this question: yes and no. One of these has to be the really correct (and not just believed to be correct) answer, even though philosophers throughout history don't agree on which it is.

It is worth noting that a similar situation arises in discussions of other controversial topics, even in science. For example, ornithopaleontologists (scientists who study the evolution of birds) apparently disagree on the correct answer to the question "Are birds the descendants of dinosaurs?" Some of them say yes; others say no. They can't both be correct even though they all *think* they're correct. The situation in this respect is analogous to that of philosophers who disagree about the possibility of after-death survival. But nobody would therefore suppose that because of the disagreement of honest, equally well trained scientists who have studied the issue, there just is no really correct answer. The advantage of scientific investigation over philosophical inquiry is that scientists at least agree on a proper method of how to go about answering scientific questions—for example, on what kind of evidence would count in favor of the truth of a hypothesis. (Another advantage is that, unlike the answers to many philosophical questions, the answers to many scientific questions have no bearing on how you should live.) But the question "What is the correct method of deciding whether a philosophical claim is true?" is itself a philosophical question, which has been answered in various (incompatible) ways throughout history.

The Pervasiveness of Philosophical Views

PHILOSOPHY IS DIFFERENT FROM ANY OF THE OTHER AREAS OF thought you will study in college, in an interesting way. This difference has to do with the nature of philosophical questions. It is possible to avoid, say, the answers to questions that arise in the study of geometry, American history, physics, or English literature. But you can't even get started in the study of all the subjects you will pursue unless you take for granted what are intrinsically philosophical assumptions.

For example, consider physics and chemistry. Physicists and chemists make the following assumptions:

- Some events cause other events.
- The physical universe operates according to fundamental laws of nature.
- Past experience of the behavior of physical objects is a reliable indicator of how physical objects will behave in similar circumstances in the future.
- We now know more about the nature of physical reality than anyone knew a thousand years ago.

Physicists and chemists assume that there is such a thing as causation, that there are laws of nature, that the physical objects will behave in the future as they have in the past, and that they as scientists have some knowledge of how physical objects work. And each of these assumptions raises questions *that cannot be answered within physics and chemistry.* For example:

- What is causation? What does it mean for one thing to cause another?
- What is a law of nature?

Suppose the following universal generalization is true: *All male corporate accountants at noon on weekdays in downtown Atlanta wear ties.* Why isn't this a law of nature? To answer, you have to think hard about the meaning of the term *law of nature,* relying on the understanding of laws of nature acquired through your study of science. You can't see with your eyes or hear with your ears or, for that matter, perceive with any of your senses that it isn't a law of nature. If you want an answer, you have no alternative but to philosophize.

Consider this question:

- How do we justify the view that physical objects in the future will behave as they have in the past?

How do we know that we are not, in fact, in the position of the farmer's chicken who reasons as follows: "The farmer has always fed me daily in the past. Therefore, he will always do so in the future." By the time the chicken gets her head whacked off, she has propagated this view to her offspring.

Finally, some questions are raised by scientists' assumption that they know what they think they do:

- What is knowledge?
- What is scientific knowledge?
- How is scientific knowledge to be distinguished from other varieties of knowledge?

You cannot construct an experiment or make observations to answer any of these questions because they aren't questions about the way the physical universe behaves; they fall outside the domain of empirical investigation. Science ultimately answers questions, at least in part, by an appeal to observations, and these questions are not about observable entities. They are about the nature or justification of abstract and theoretical ideas.

If you say that, because of the abstract nature of these questions, there really aren't any answers (or any correct answers) because the questions can't be answered by scientific—that is, observational—means, then you are merely taking the following view for granted:

(P1) Only those questions decidable by sense experience have answers.

Yet P1 is itself a philosophical principle whose truth cannot be decided by sense experience. If we ask, "Is P1 true?" then, according to P1, there can't be an answer to that question. This rather pulls the rug out from under anyone who thinks that the principle is true. We could point out to such a person that he ought not to believe P1, because on its own grounds its truth cannot be determined.

Now consider history. Your history professor or the author of your textbook will probably assume that the correct way to represent time graphically is as a line, going from earlier to later, and not as a circle such that historical events repeat themselves eternally. However, if we ask why history should or must be represented as a line instead of as a circle, the question cannot be answered by historical research but only by philosophical reflection.

Or suppose you take a course in psychology, in which you study the famous Harvard psychologist B. F. Skinner. According to Skinner, the object of study for psychology is observable human behavior, not unobservable mental states. In fact, many philosophers take Skinner to hold a view of the nature of mind known as philosophical behaviorism. According to this view, to say that you are in pain means that you are behaving in a certain observable fashion or are disposed to behave some observable way. Once your behavior is described, there is nothing more to say about your pain. Is Skinner correct? You can't devise a research project with rats or humans to find out because his view concerns an abstract unobservable—namely, the concept of pain or, more generally, how we are to understand the nature of human minds. To decide whether he's correct, you need to think hard about the reasons he offers to support his view and see whether you can discover any reasons to reject it.

Skinner and many of his behaviorist colleagues also have thought that because all human behavior is—at least in principle—predictable on the basis of determining causes, there is no interesting sense in which human beings have free will. Is he correct? To decide, you'll again have to investigate the reasons available for and against the existence of free will. Of course, you're going to have to begin by getting a good conceptual handle on how we're to understand the ideas of determinism and free will.

Traditionally, psychology is the study of the workings of the human mind. But what is the mind? Is it identical to the brain? Why or why not? This point can't be decided by experiment alone, because the answer in part depends on what you mean by "identity" and the fact (if it is a fact) that the mind is identical to the brain is not an *observable* fact. (Which isn't to say that observations are not relevant to deciding the issue.)

Philosophy Is Everywhere

It would be easy to continue this survey. We can look at every intellectual discipline and discover philosophical answers that are being presupposed to philosophical questions that cannot be answered within the disciplines themselves. These assumptions provide the intellectual scaffolding without which those working in the disciplines could not proceed. If we inquire into the meaning or truth of these assumptions, we're going to have to philosophize.

Here are some other examples:

Discipline	Philosophical Questions
Mathematics	• Do numbers exist?
	• Is mathematics discovered or invented?
Biology	• What is a species?
	• What is the connection between biological explanations and chemical explanations?
	• What is a biological function?
Economics	• What is rationality?
	• What reasons are there for treating corporations like quasi-persons?
	• Does the "rational" person always act selfishly?
Languages	• How does language relate to the world?
	• How do words hook onto things?
	• What is meaning?

Religion	• What are miracles, are they possible, and what sort of evidence would you need to know that one has occurred?
	• What is the relation between faith and reason?
	• Is reincarnation possible?
	• Is there a God?
Political Science	• Is a caring society preferable to a just one?
	• What is a just society?
	• Can we be said to "own" ourselves?

Philosophical Questions

I AM NOT GOING TO PRESENT YOU WITH A HARD AND FAST DEFINI-tion of what a question must be like to qualify as a philosophical question. I don't have any such definition, any more than I have a definition of what an activity must be to qualify as a game. Nevertheless, just as I still know how to tell the difference between a game and a nongame, I can say something useful about distinguishing philosophical questions from other kinds of questions.

A good place to start is to see whether a question has any features that disqualify it from the philosophical arena. Consider the following questions:

- Does gold dissolve in hydrochloric acid?
- Are birds descended from dinosaurs?

- How old is the universe?
- Did Napoleon win at Waterloo?
- Are professional artists more or less depressive than the general population?
- Is sexual orientation genetically determined?
- What is the connection between interest rates and inflation?
- Who is the fastest living sprinter in the world?
- Is there any mustard in the refrigerator?

None of these questions is an intrinsically philosophical question. The way to find the answer to most of them is to investigate according to the method of the relevant empirical science. One is a historical question. Several questions merely require common sense and ordinary powers of observation to get the answer. In each case, empirical evidence is key. If no one can see the mustard in the fridge, it isn't there.

But the evidence may not be so obviously decisive. Contrary to a view widespread among the scientifically illiterate, scientific investigation is rarely just a matter of "look and see." Scientists familiar with the same body of evidence may disagree on how to interpret the evidence. That's why the answers to the questions about the descent of birds and the age of the universe are still controversial in paleontology and astrophysics. Even so, scientists can usually at least imagine the kind of observations that would answer such questions and resolve the controversy. Future empirical evidence *could* be decisive, even if the present evidence is not.

Philosophical questions, however, cannot be answered on the basis of sense observation alone. This is not to say that empirical evidence is always irrelevant to the answers to these questions. In fact, empirical evidence can count against a philosophical view. For example, if someone held the unlikely view that mental happenings are always and everywhere unrelated to physical happenings, then slapping themselves on the cheek would provide them with some reason to think otherwise.

Insofar as philosophical questions are not decidable by observation alone, they are like other theoretical questions with which we are familiar. For example, consider the following question: What kind of evidence would count strongly in favor of the claim that a cure for AIDS has been discovered? You won't be able to answer this question by using your five senses. You'll need to think hard, using your understanding of the disease and your judgment of the possibilities, combined with a lot of background knowledge about the way things work in the world. Or consider this question: Does Einstein's Special Theory of Relativity show that our ordinary view of time is incorrect? Again, you can't use your five senses to answer. There's no substitute here for hard thinking, beginning with an attempt to understand the Special Theory and our "ordinary view" of time.

Not that theoretical judgments are always or even usually difficult. You won't have to think long about the answer to the theoretical question, if you're thinking of buying a used car, of whether you should trust the advice of an experienced car mechanic or the advice of a friend who doesn't know the difference between an alternator and a carburetor. Even though this is intrinsically a theoretical question, nobody thinks that there is not a correct answer, and most of us think we know what that answer is.

Look again at the list of questions. Each question addresses a specific issue in a specific field or in daily experience. However, a characteristic of many philosophical questions is that they are very *general*. The ornithopaleontologist may ask whether anyone knows or is justified in believing that birds are descended from dinosaurs. Philosophers have asked whether anyone knows or is justified in believing *anything at all*. Astrophysicists have asked whether there is any good evidence for the existence of black holes. Philosophers have asked what, in general, distinguishes good evidence from bad evidence. It is just assumed by the various sciences that scientific knowledge and rational judgments are possible, in order to get on with the business of science. The view that we cannot know or reasonably believe anything is known as *skepticism*. It is a characteristically philosophical question to ask whether and how knowledge or rational belief is possible at all.

One of philosophy's traditional projects has been the attempt to better understand the *concepts* we employ in our beliefs about reality. Some philosophers have even held that this task of getting clear on what we mean—of clarifying our concepts—is the principal task of philosophy. This project gives rise to such characteristically philosophical questions as the following: What is goodness? What is consciousness? What distinguishes knowledge from mere true belief? What is the self? What is justice? What is happiness?

Other characteristically philosophical questions arise when we focus on the justification of our fundamental beliefs about the world. Many people believe that there is a God who created and sustains the physical universe. Others assume that the physical universe is all there is. Many of us assume that human beings are responsible for their actions in virtue of their possession of what we call "free will." Others deny this. Most of us think that some actions are right and some actions are wrong. Others say that this is a distinction without a difference based on personal taste and upbringing, so that statements such as "Infanticide is wrong" are never true. To ask whether any of these views is rationally defensible is to ask a characteristically philosophical question.

CHAPTER 4

Assertion, Belief, and Truth

PEOPLE HAVE BELIEFS. SOME PEOPLE BELIEVE THAT OSWALD acted alone. Others believe that there was a conspiracy behind the assassination of Kennedy. Some people believe that the physical universe is teeming with extraterrestrial life in faraway places. Others disagree. You could no doubt easily fill a page with a list of sentences that begin with the words "I believe. . . ."

But how are we to understand this fact? What does it mean to say that somebody has a belief? What is involved in believing? And how is believing related to other things we are or do? A good place to start answering these questions is to reflect on how we use language to *express* our beliefs. Of course, language can be used in many other ways. We ask questions: "Would you please shut the door?" We give orders and make requests: "Turn the volume down!" We also sometimes use language merely to express emotion, such as when you accidentally hit your thumb with a hammer. In none of these cases does it make sense for someone standing by to say, "Oh, I agree," or "That's not correct," or "You've got that right," because we have not said anything that can be agreed or disagreed with, that is the case or not.

At other times, however, we use language to make assertions by which we intend to communicate information. For example:

- "The cat is on the mat."
- "The sun is a large ball of burning gases."
- "Every even number is the sum of two primes."

When we make assertions, we are stating what we think about the way things were, are, or will be. We are saying what we think is the case. And it makes perfectly good sense (even if it is not reasonable) for someone who hears us to agree or disagree. What they agree or disagree with is what we have said, which needn't be said in English, of course. All of the following sentences assert the same thing: "*Es schneit*"; "*Il neige*"; "It is snowing." The "same thing" they all say is what philosophers usually call a *proposition*. The proposition is the message. Different languages are merely the medium by which the message is embodied and expressed. Thus, the same proposition can be expressed by assertions spoken or written in different languages.

When we make assertions, we express our beliefs, or represent ourselves as doing so. Suppose that someone spoke the following two sentences to you: "The Earth orbits around the sun" and "I do not believe that the Earth orbits around the sun." This makes no sense. The first assertion is not about the speaker; it is about the Earth and sun. However, if it is an assertion (so not spoken with intent to deceive), we understand that the speaker believes what she has said.

Whenever you have a belief, it always makes sense to ask what it is you believe. Beliefs have a special "about-ness": it isn't possible just to have a belief, like having an itch or a headache, because a "belief" is always a "belief that _____." What fills in the blank is the expression of the proposition believed. In other words, each belief has a specific content that distinguishes it from other beliefs. For example, my belief that Morehouse College is in Atlanta (which I express when I say or write "Morehouse College is in Atlanta") differs from my belief that Morehouse is not in Los Angeles.

Believing and Intellectual Commitment

But there is more. Belief carries an unavoidable intellectual commitment to the truth of what you believe. For example, if I believe that dinosaurs are extinct, then I have an intellectual stance on the truth of the following statement: "Dinosaurs are extinct." I contradict myself if I say, "I believe that dinosaurs are extinct and the proposition *Dinosaurs are extinct* is false." To believe that cows cannot fly is to commit yourself to a yes answer to the question "Is it true that cows cannot fly?" You are going out on a limb, intellectually speaking, every time you have a belief.

Note that we're talking here about *having* a belief, not the act of *claiming* to believe something. To have a belief is to have a tendency to assent to the truth of what you believe, to say yes to the proposition you believe were you to consider whether it says what is so. There are degrees of intellectual commitment, and we often tell someone that we "believe" such and such to express the fact that we don't think we know it with absolute certainty. Sometimes "I believe . . ." may mean "I'm not sure." ("I believe there are no indigenous rodents in New Zealand, but maybe not.") Sometimes "I believe . . ." means, "I find it useful and/or moving to say this, but in so saying I'm not making an assertion." ("I believe the Atlanta Braves will win their division this year.") Nevertheless, you can't eliminate your intellectual commitment to the truth of what you believe—if you do in fact believe it—by saying, "That's just *my* belief." Of course, believing that something is the case doesn't make it the case.

The intellectual commitment built into your own beliefs is highlighted by the following fact. You can report someone else's beliefs without endorsing what they believe, but you cannot play this same game with yourself. You can treat someone else's belief as a mere psychological fact about them and remain intellectually neutral about the proposition they believe. You cannot report your own beliefs without endorsing what you believe, thereby committing yourself to the truth of the proposition you believe. For example, a book on evolutionary medicine is sitting on the shelf beside me, a book I look forward to reading, in part because I know so very little about the field. I am now picking the book up, opening it at random to a page near the back. On that page the author tells us, "The molecular mimicry hypothesis for ankylosing spondilitis and other rheumatologic disorders has some experimental support." At present I have no idea what the "molecular mimicry hypothesis" is, but this provides no obstacle to my reporting the author's belief that the hypothesis—whatever he means by it—has experimental support. There's no contradiction if I say, "The author believes the molecular mimicry hypothesis has some experimental support, but I don't believe it does" as there is if I say "I believe the molecular mimicry hypothesis has some experimental support, but I don't think there is any experimental support for the hypothesis." Likewise, there's no contradiction if I say, "Lots of people believe that there are UFOs, but I don't think there are any UFOs," as there is if I say "I believe there are UFOs, but I don't think there are any."

Objective Reality

I have so far used the terms *true* and *false* without defining them. Our assertions express our beliefs, and to have a belief is to be committed to the truth of some proposition. (Note that I have been careful not to say that to have a belief always involves believing that some proposition is true, because someone—for example, a small child—can have beliefs without possessing the concept of truth at all.) But what makes a proposition true?

Before I can answer this question, I need to introduce one more idea: the idea of objective reality. You've already got this idea, whether you realize it or not. It is hard to see how we can think about ourselves or anything else without assuming that there is something that answers to the phrase "what is the case." Indeed, the idea is simply inescapable if we are going to think at all. You understand the distinction between "the way things appear" and "the way things really are." For example, on a hot day in summer the highway may appear wet in the distance, when in fact it is dry. The full moon in the sky appears to the naked eye to be the size of a quarter held at arm's length, but it is really a massive globe. "Objective reality" is just "whatever is the case" or "the way things really are," independently of how things may appear to anyone, and independently of what anyone may think is the case.

It is easy to get confused about the idea of objective reality, especially if you are familiar with discussions in terms of "my reality" and "your reality." "There is no objective reality," someone objects. "There is only my reality and your reality. My reality may include God and angels. Yours may not. But each of us has the only 'reality' there is for anyone." This contention has an initial appeal to a lot of people. But its force depends on collapsing the distinction between objective reality and beliefs about objective reality—the distinction between what *is* the case and what is *believed* to be the case. The objector pretty clearly is taking "my reality" to mean "my beliefs about reality" and is objecting to the idea of objective reality on the grounds that people disagree about what is real.

However, to say that there is an objective reality—a "what is the case"—is not to say that anyone's beliefs accurately describe that reality. Indeed, the point is simply that what is real is independent of our conceptions of it. You probably remember as a child shaking a gift-wrapped box that contained your birthday present to see whether you could guess what was in the box. Your idea of "the thing in the box" before getting it out is rather like the idea of objective reality. Any number of things could be in the box, and so many guesses make sense. But all the guesses can't be correct. Objective reality could be any number of ways, and those ways are described in alternative conceptions. But all the conceptions can't be correct.

The Definition of Truth

Now for a definition: *A proposition is true if and only if objective reality is the way that the proposition says it is; otherwise, the proposition is false.* For example, the proposition expressed by "The cat is on the mat" is true just in case objective reality is such that (or, simply, it is the case that) the cat is on the mat. "The Pyramids are older than the Washington Monument" is true just in case objective reality is such that the Pyramids are older than the Washington Monument. The proposition expressed by "No hydrogen atom is identical to a uranium atom" is true just in case objective reality is such that no hydrogen atom is identical to a uranium atom. The proposition expressed by "You, the reader, have two brothers and no sisters" is true just in case it is the case that you have two brothers and no sisters.

Notice that all this is not going to help you find out which propositions are true or false. Knowing what makes something you believe true or false isn't going to help you if your question is "How can I *tell* whether this particular belief of mine is true?" or "How can I tell whether something I don't presently believe is true or false?" These very important questions were never supposed to be answered by a characterization of truth and falsity. In this respect, the idea of truth is like the idea of "the undiscovered species of beetles in Brazil." Having the idea by itself doesn't instruct you on how best to proceed in finding out which things the idea applies to. But the idea is presupposed by the search. Unless it is possible that undiscovered species of beetles live in Brazil, there is no point in looking for them. And unless true beliefs may exist, there is no point in trying to answer the question "How can I tell whether a proposition is true?"

What about the commonly heard pronouncement that something is "true for me"? If this phrase merely means (as I think it usually does) that the speaker believes something, and so believes that it is true, then the expression "true for me" is misleading but innocuous. In fact, this is merely a way of acknowledging the intellectual commitment involved when someone has a belief. However, sometimes it is clear that people who use this expression intend to be telling us something about the nature of truth. "What I mean by the term *true*," they might say, "is merely 'true for me.'" This won't do, because we can always ask them what they mean by *true* in "true for me." If they say they mean "true for me," then the same question arises again. Unless we finally get to a characterization of "true" that illuminates the term and doesn't just use it over again, we will never get an answer to the question.

For these reasons, it is perhaps best to eschew the expression "true for me" altogether and replace it with something such as "in my opinion, true" or "what I believe." Still, sometimes the expression seems an apt way to express what you think is an intrinsically personal attitude or taste that you don't expect or care that other people adopt, as in "It's true for me that my wife is the most beautiful woman in the world."

I have also heard it argued that the ideas of truth and objective reality should be rejected on moral and political grounds. The argument begins with the claim that throughout history people who have believed in objective reality and "Truth with a capital *T*" have always tried to force their views on other people who do not agree with them. Such intellectual imperialism, the argument runs, is wrong. Therefore, to avoid such morally wrong behavior ourselves, we should jettison the ideas of objective reality and truth. The problem with the argument is that it makes no sense at all unless the historical and moral claims it makes are true in the very sense of "truth" that the argument is supposed to lead us to reject. Unless historical reality—that is, what is the case historically—is objectively the way the arguer says it is (whatever anyone may think), then there is nothing left to argue from. And unless it is true that intellectual imperialism is wrong (even if someone doesn't think it is true), the argument collapses. In short, we have to believe that the reasons offered in support of the conclusion are *true* to consider them reasons for the conclusion that denies this.

Subjectivism and Conventionalism

People attracted to this argument have mistakenly supposed that anyone who accepts the idea of an objective reality is saying that *their* views are the only ones that could be true. Interestingly, the exact opposite is the case. To recognize that what makes your beliefs true is not merely that you believe them is to admit the possibility of error, for reality must "cooperate" with you to have a true belief. Of course, this will make no sense to someone who collapses the distinction between what is believed and having a belief. Unfortunately, two widely held (or at least widely touted) views do just that.

The first view is *subjectivism*. The subjectivist's motto is "All truth is subjective." The subjectivist rejects (or at least purports to reject) the notion of an objective reality—a way things are—that determines the truth or falsity of beliefs. Truth, says the subjectivist, has nothing to do with anything outside the believing agent; it is a purely subjective feature of someone's beliefs. Thus, when someone says, "It is true that there are ghosts," it is a mistake to think they are talking about anything but their own subjective psychological makeup. They are telling you something about themselves, not about ghosts, just as they would be telling you something about their own subjective constitution, and not beer, were they to say "I like the taste of beer." In other words, if you ask of a belief, "Is it true?" the subjectivist says you must first ask, "For whom?" Each individual has his or her own "truths," which is why all truth is relative to individuals, and has nothing to do with "objective reality."

Consider again the subjectivist's claim "All truth is subjective." Suppose we ask whether it is true, and so something we should believe. Well, there are only two possibilities: it must be true objectively or subjectively. It can't be true objectively—that is, it can't tell us what is objectively the case, the way things really are—for then it would be false if true. In this respect, it would be like the sentence "Nothing correct has ever been written in English." But it can't be true merely subjectively, for this would mean that it is a mere autobiographical piece of information about the subjectivist (such as "I'm sick"), a fact that does not at all rule out the correctness of its denial (that is, the claim that all truth is *not* subjective).

Although one hardly needs a further reason to reject subjectivism, let me mention one other difficulty, since the same difficulty arises with the second view I'm going to discuss. Subjectivists abhor the notions of nonrelative truth and nonrelative reality, and they object to the idea of objective reality that I have used in defining truth. Yet subjectivism is an account that cannot even be stated unless the following claim is true in the very way the subjectivist denies that anything can be true: There are persons who have beliefs. Unless this claim describes the way things really are—that is, provides us with a nonrelative truth about a nonrelative reality—the subjectivist has no account to offer. Which is just to say that the subjectivist can't really get away with rejecting the ideas of objective reality and truth. Thus, again, if subjectivism is correct, then it must be mistaken.

You may not know any simple subjectivists, but the next view is sure to ring a familiar bell. I will call it "conventionalism," because it gives pride of place to social convention in its account of truth. According to the conventionalist, there is no reality existing independently of the societies or cultures developed by human beings. The idea of an objective reality "out there" waiting to be discovered is empty. Different societies do not *discover* reality. Rather, reality is constructed or invented by each society, which has its own "truths" and its own standards for determining what ought to be thought. Moreover, this socially constructed "reality" can only be assessed in its own terms. If you ask of a belief, "Is it true?" the conventionalist says you can't answer without knowing the answer to "For which society?"

Conventionalism is, I think, partly motivated by the realization that we all need a tradition to provide us with a platform from which to deal with reality. We all depend on some particular background of concepts and beliefs. We never meet reality in the raw, devoid of any preconceptions. For example, consider your belief that water is H_2O. This is not a belief that anyone living thousands of years ago could have had. From the perspective of someone living in, say, ancient Greece or India, reality did not contain chemical elements or molecules. Their beliefs about reality did not include such items. They, unlike us, did not have the theoretical wherewithal needed to understand the idea of water's molecular structure. But none of this provides any reason to reject the idea of an objective reality that is discovered, not invented. Changes in belief about reality don't require changes in reality.

Why conventionalism is so appealing to some contemporary intellectuals is an interesting question that I won't pursue. I will simply call your attention to the fact that conventionalism seems to fall foul of the same problem as subjectivism. For the conventionalist's picture is clearly put forward as itself a fact about the world, a fact that exists whether or not it is recognized by all societies. Consider the conventionalist's belief that there are human societies. Notice that this belief could not even be held or expressed in most societies throughout history, for their members lacked the social science concept of a "society." However, it is pretty clear that conventionalists take their belief accurately to describe the way things really are, independent of how anyone conceives things to be. Thus, unless at least *this* belief is true in the society-independent way that the conventionalist says *no* belief can be true, the conventionalist has no account to offer. But if the conventionalist's account involves such non-relatively true beliefs, then conventionalism is false. As with subjectivism, to hold the view as a serious intellectual stance is at the same time to possess a conclusive reason to reject it.

One final comment on subjectivism and conventionalism, views that object to the notion of nonrelative truth and the correlative idea of objective reality. It is hard to see how either of these relativistic views can make sense of the following thoughts:

- Believing (either individually or corporately) typically does not make it so.
- We can have false beliefs that we will never discover to be false.
- There are many truths about the world that we will never know and have no way of finding out.
- If a belief is true, it typically would be true even if no one believed it.
- It is possible to doubt whether your own view of reality or your society's view of reality is true.

If these thoughts make sense to you, you have good reason to reject the relativist's suggestion that truth, belief, and reality are indistinguishable categories.

Degrees of Belief

Although truth and falsity, like pregnancy and extinction, do not come in degrees, our beliefs do come in varying degrees of strength. For example, my belief that Atlanta is more than one hundred miles from Chicago is much stronger than my belief that I will live to be over seventy years old. My belief that sugar dissolves in boiling water is stronger than my belief that most of the spiders I see are females.

Because of this feature of beliefs, we can always ask two questions about the reasonableness of someone's belief that some proposition (call it "P") is true: (1) Is it reasonable for them to believe that P at all? and (2) Is it reasonable for them to believe that P to the degree that they do? For example, suppose I buy 501 tickets in a lottery I know has only 1,000 tickets. Even if it is reasonable for me to believe that I will win, it is certainly unreasonable for me to believe this very strongly. If I buy 900 of the tickets, then it may be reasonable for me to believe very strongly that I will win, but still not reasonable to believe with absolute certainty.

On Concepts

EACH OF US HAS A MENTAL MAP OF THE WORLD, A REPRESENTA-
tion that consists, in part, of an extraordinarily complex
web of interrelated beliefs about the way things are. If we
want to understand our beliefs and the assertions that express them, we need to focus on the ideas or concepts
underlying our thinking and speaking. To understand
the concept of, say, a horse or an electron is to understand what we mean when we use the terms *horse* and
electron.

It may seem somewhat foolish to consider what we
mean by such garden-variety terms as *table, chair, tree,* or
dog. Don't we all already know what we're talking about
when we use these words? Well, yes, we do, and we had

better, since learning the conventional meanings of such ordinary terms is part of learning a natural language such as English. We can all cite clear examples of objects to which such words properly apply, and we also know that you can't successfully use the word *tree* to refer in English to just any kind of object.

But even in nonphilosophical discourse, it is easy to imagine circumstances in which the meaning of a term (or the understanding of a concept) may be important. Suppose the city creates a new ordinance that says that no trees are allowed within ten yards of fire hydrants. If I have a fifteen-foot-tall persimmon bush next to the fire hydrant in my front yard, it may be important to me to learn what concept of a tree is operative in the ordinance. (In this case, the city will probably just stipulate some definition of the term *tree* for ordinance purposes.)

Understanding gets more difficult when we move into the area of abstract concepts. Consider, for example, the concept of a physical object. What are we talking about when we talk about physical objects? You might think that this issue can be decided by merely opening the dictionary. It can't. Here is the *American Heritage Dictionary*'s definition of the word *physical*: "Of or pertaining to the body, as distinguished from the mind or spirit; bodily; corporeal." OK, then, but this definition doesn't shed much light. Part of the problem is that it defines *physical* by merely telling us what a physical thing is not: it is not, or doesn't pertain to, mind or spirit. And what do those terms mean? Or consider *bodily* and *corporeal*. Neither a gravitational field, the weak nuclear force, visible light, nor ultraviolet radiation seems to be bodily or corporeal—at least not in the way Tiger Woods's golf clubs or the Sears Tower clearly are. So are these items studied by physicists not really physical objects?

Consider the concept of God. Whether you deny or affirm the existence of God, presumably you have some idea of the sort of being whose existence you're affirming or denying. When the first Soviet cosmonauts orbited the globe, they radioed down that they had not seen God. Apparently, they thought that they were somehow providing evidence against the views of Christians, Jews, and Muslims. However, they obviously didn't understand the classical concept of God, for if they had, they would have realized that seeing God from their space capsule would have *refuted,* not *confirmed,* traditional theism.

Finally, consider such familiar terms as *knowledge, memory, justice,* and *science.* What does it mean to know? What distinguishes a genuine memory from a merely apparent memory? What is justice? Why isn't astrology a genuine science? Is backward time travel possible? What is causation, and can an effect precede its cause? To inquire into the answers to such questions, you've got to decide how these terms should best be understood (which may be only distantly related to how the word is currently used).

Sufficient and Necessary Conditions

Philosophers have developed a useful intellectual tool to investigate questions of meaning. They seek to find the "conditions for the proper application of a concept," which thereby provide a key to the correct understanding of the concept for which the term stands. There are two kinds of conditions: sufficient conditions and necessary conditions.

A sufficient condition tells you something about an item that, if true of the item, is enough to allow you to apply the concept to that item. Being a tree, for example, is a sufficient condition of something's being a plant. So, if the concept "tree" applies to an object, this is enough to guarantee that the concept "plant" does too. Being a desire is a sufficient condition of something's being a psychological state. So if the concept "desire" applies to an item, this is enough to guarantee that the concept "psychological state" does too.

Suppose you want to find a *sufficient condition* for the proper application of the concept of a fish. Here is a simple strategy. Consider the following statement:

> If the concept of a _____ applies to X, then the concept of a fish applies to X (in other words, X is a fish).

Now try to find concepts that will fill in the blank and make this statement true. Well, the concepts of a trout, a barracuda, and a swordfish do the job. So a sufficient condition of being a fish is being a trout, being a barracuda, being a swordfish, or indeed being any other species of fish.

A *necessary condition* tells you something about an item that must be true of the item to apply the relevant concept to that item. For example, consider our concept of treehood. Nothing can be a tree that is not also a plant. No object that is not a plant is a tree. So, if we cannot say of an object that it is a plant, then, given this connection between the concepts of treehood and planthood, we cannot call it a tree, either. Being a plant is a necessary condition of being a tree.

Again, there is a simple strategy that you can use. Suppose you want to find necessary conditions for the proper application of the concept of a vacuum cleaner. What you need to find is something that completes the following statement and makes it true:

> If the concept of a vacuum cleaner applies to X (that is, if X is a vacuum cleaner), then the concept of a _____ applies to X.

What must something be to qualify as a vacuum cleaner? Well, it must be an object designed to clean up household dirt. So, being an object designed for cleaning up household dirt is a necessary condition of being a vacuum cleaner. But it is not also a sufficient condition, for the following statement is false:

> If X is an object designed to clean up household dirt,
> then X is a vacuum cleaner.

You can see that this statement is false when you realize that mops and brooms are also objects designed to clean up household dirt.

You may have figured out that there is a mutual relation between necessary and sufficient conditions. Anytime you find one, you also have found another. Consider the concepts of two kinds of objects, Xs and Ys. If being an X is a sufficient condition of being a Y, then being a Y is a necessary condition of being an X. For example, being an apple is a sufficient condition of being a fruit, and being a fruit is a necessary condition of being an apple. Note that being a fruit is not a sufficient condition of being an apple because the concept of fruithood applies to oranges and bananas, too.

Sometimes, if you discover enough necessary conditions for the application of a concept, you will also have a sufficient condition. Your understanding of a concept will be much enhanced if you find such "jointly sufficient and necessary conditions." The concept of a bachelor provides a good illustration. Being unmarried is a necessary condition of being a bachelor, as is being male. Neither condition alone is sufficient for the application of the concept of a bachelor, but together they provide jointly sufficient and necessary conditions for someone's being a bachelor.

Here, too, a simple strategy is available. Suppose you want to find jointly sufficient and necessary conditions for the proper application of the concept of a widow. What you need to find is some same thing that fills each of the following statements and makes both statements true:

1. If the concept of a widow applies to X (that is, if X is a widow), then the concept of a _____ applies to X.
2. If the concept of a _____ applies to X, then the concept of a widow applies to X.

In this case, "woman who has a deceased husband" will do the job.

You are going to have to use your imagination and background knowledge to determine when and whether a proposed sufficient or necessary condition for the application of a concept is indeed just that. This is where counterexamples come in. Successful counterexamples are knockdown objections to conceptual proposals, so they play an important role in philosophizing. Suppose someone proposes that having a brain is a sufficient condition of having mathematical thoughts. If you can think of anything that has a brain but does not have mathematical thoughts, then you will have found a counterexample to the proposal. Well, can you? Here are two animals that fit the bill: roaches and toads. They have brains, but no mathematical thoughts. So the conceptual proposal is mistaken.

Or suppose someone says that having a functioning biological brain is a necessary condition of having a mind. This is a controversial claim, but let me give you two examples of what have been taken to be counterexamples to it. First, some philosophers think that they can imagine a thinking computer built entirely from mechanical parts. If such a machine is coherently imaginable, then it must be possible, and something can have a mind without having a biological brain. Second, some philosophers think that they can imagine their minds or selves existing without their bodies. Again, if this is a coherent possibility, then the connection between having a brain and having a mind is not a necessary connection. As these examples show, counterexamples themselves can be controversial when difficult philosophical issues are at stake.

Note also that, when we are thinking about the proper understanding of a concept, we are interested in the question of what objects or items a concept could properly apply to, and not merely the question of what items the concept in fact does apply to. For example, suppose you decide that the concept of a "person" is best defined as the concept of a "rational agent." Even if you think that the only rational agents in existence are human beings— that is, members of the terrestrial species *Homo sapiens*—it would be a mistake to conclude that the concept of a person is just the concept of a human being. For this would mean that, were it to turn out that intelligent extraterrestrials like those found in science fiction really exist, you wouldn't be able to call them "persons," even though they would certainly be rational agents.

Philosophical "definitions" are often cast in the form of (or at least implicitly provide one with) a set of jointly sufficient and necessary conditions for the application of a concept. Such definitions are best viewed as recommendations of how a concept is best understood philosophically; thus, they share the controversial nature of all substantive philosophical stances. Evaluating such definitions is the bread and butter of much philosophizing.

I want to give you two more examples to illustrate how useful the scrutiny of sufficient and necessary conditions can be. Recall the philosophical behaviorism held by many Skinnerian psychologists. According to this view, our concept of pain is the concept of behaving in specifiable publicly observable ways (grimacing, saying "Ouch!" and so on); there is nothing more to pain than these public displays. In terms of necessary and sufficient conditions, the philosophical behaviorist is saying that behaving in certain observable ways is both a sufficient and a necessary condition of a person's (say, Orville's) being in pain. If this is so, then the following statements must be true:

1. If Orville grimaces, says "Oh, it hurts!" and writhes in the appropriate way, then Orville is in pain.
2. If Orville is in pain, then Orville grimaces, says "Oh, it hurts!" and writhes in the appropriate way.

Well, can we imagine circumstances that would make either 1 or 2 false? Can we, in other words, find counterexamples to this account of pain? Easily. Orville can act like he is in pain even though he isn't. So 1 doesn't provide a sufficient condition of being in pain. And 2 doesn't provide a necessary condition, because Orville can be in pain (for example, have a headache) even though he does not express his pain in any publicly observable fashion. The falsity of 1 and 2 sheds light on the fundamental flaw in philosophical behaviorism: It attempts to characterize mental states such as pain without appeal to the subjective experiences that are essential to such states.

Now for my second example: the concept of knowledge. A redoubtable tradition holds that propositional knowledge (knowledge that something is the case) should be defined in terms of the following jointly sufficient and necessary conditions (Let "S" be a person and "P" a proposition):

  i. S believes that P;
 ii. S is justified in believing that P; and
iii. P is true.

This is the "justified true belief" account of knowledge.

This account is widely regarded as inadequate because of the following sort of counterexample. Suppose I go for a drive in the Vermont countryside. Unbeknownst to me, some local farmers have decided to play a joke on city-slicker tourists. They have erected in their pastures, several hundred yards from the road, numerous facades of barns. Suppose that one of these facades renders an actual barn directly behind it unviewable from the road. I don't know this, nor do I know about the other numerous facades. Thus, when I take a Sunday drive and see this facade in this distance, the following are true:

1. I believe that there is a barn in the pasture beside the road;
2. I am justified in believing that there is a barn in the pasture beside the road; and
3. it is true that there is a barn in the pasture beside the road.

In short, all of the conditions i, ii, and iii are satisfied, yet it seems obvious that I do not know that there is a barn beside the road. Therefore, the three proposed conditions do not together provide a sufficient condition of propositional knowledge.

Notice that the success of this counterexample depends on two factors. First, there is the imaginative construction of circumstances in which the conditions are met. Second, there is the intuition or insight that knowledge of the relevant propositions isn't part of the picture. Without this intuition, no philosopher would consider the story a counterexample. The intuition needn't be expressed with the word *intuition,* however. We could have as well said that "it makes no sense" or "it is absurd" or "it seems plainly false" to say that I have the relevant bit of knowledge on my Sunday drive.

Without such intuitive judgments, it would be impossible to realize that you have hit on a counterexample to a view. So it is hardly surprising that here is one place your intuitions are going to be important when you philosophize. Of course, our intuitions can be overturned in the process of philosophizing. It may turn out that the intuitions generated by our nonreflective concept of such and such will not stand up under scrutiny. (According to many philosophers, such death by scrutiny is the fate of our ordinary "intuition" that time is constantly "flowing" from the past into the future.) Nevertheless, our philosophizing should always be answerable to these intuitions, because they count among the clearest things we think we understand or grasp at all.

Conceptual Distinctions

So much for sufficient and necessary conditions. In concluding this chapter, I'd like to consider another obvious way in which thinking about concepts enters into philosophizing. It is hard to imagine philosophizing or any other sort of theorizing that does not rely heavily on the drawing of *conceptual distinctions*. For example, the Justified

True Belief account of knowledge discussed earlier is intended to illuminate the nature of propositional knowledge, whose concept is distinct from the concept of other varieties of knowledge. The concept of knowledge employed when we talk about knowing *how* to ride or knowing Bill Clinton personally is different from the concept of knowing *that* a proposition is true. Therefore, as it stands, the philosophical question "What is knowledge?" is ambiguous. To "disambiguate" the question, we need to distinguish the varieties of knowledge and specify which one is at issue.

Often you will not be able to get started with your attempt to answer a philosophical question until you have specified how you are employing key concepts. Consider a question that is relevant to philosophizing about the nature of visual perception: "Does the man hallucinating on LSD really see the purple rats climbing the walls of his house?" It is possible to answer this question both yes and no on conceptual grounds. For suppose, as many philosophers do, you draw a conceptual distinction between *seeing* and merely *having a visual experience,* such that seeing an object requires that it exists and causes your visual experience. Assuming this distinction, we can say that the hallucinating man has a visual experience of purple rats but does not see the rats.

It is always helpful to set off real distinctions with verbal distinctions to avoid confusion. For example, a lot of confusion arises when a person uses the term *fact* without defining what she means, which is why it's worth taking some time to consider the facts about facts. Let's look at two answers to the question "What is a fact?"

Answer 1: *A fact is whatever can be taken for granted by two participants in a discussion.* For clarity, let's call what is a fact in this sense an agreement-fact. Of course, there is no intrinsic connection between what is an agreement-fact and what's true and really the case, because an agreement-fact is merely a matter of what two or more persons agree about. If two or more persons accept something as noncontroversial and obvious, then it counts as an agreement-fact relative to their discourse. This sense of fact must be intended when people say such things as "It was a fact in many ancient cultures that the Earth is flat" or "It is a fact in some Latin-American subcultures that voodoo cures illnesses." To know whether something is an agreement-fact, you must first answer the question "To whom?" In this way, the concept of an agreement-fact is similar to the concept of leftness, insofar as it is what we may call a "person-relative" concept. The concept of an agreement-fact is important for the following reason: Unless there is at least some common intellectual ground between you and the person with whom you are discussing a philosophical question, the discussion will be fruitless.

Answer 2: *A fact is an objective reality, a way things are.* Call this kind of fact an "objective fact." It's clear that you can't get directly from something's being an objective fact to its being an agreement-fact, or vice versa. It has always been an objective fact that the Earth is not flat, but in some societies the flatness of the Earth was an agreement-fact. And even if the entire population of the world believed that the Earth is flat, such agreement alone could hardly make the Earth's flatness an objective fact. We need this idea of facthood to make sense of mistaken beliefs about the world and to understand the old saw "Believing it doesn't make it so." It is also the idea of facthood at work when we talk of scientists "discovering," for example, the chemical composition of water or the shape of the DNA molecule or the fundamental laws of physics. To "discover" something is to find something that is there independently of your knowing or believing that it is there. This is why there is no necessary overlap between whatever is an agreement-fact and what is an objective fact (except perhaps in the mind of God, as Stephen Hawking would say). Since we all believe that our own beliefs are true, then we all think we know a lot of objective facts. In other words, there is a necessary connection between what you believe (and so what may serve as an agreement-fact in your conversation with someone who shares your belief) and what you consider an objective fact. If you believe that leprechauns exist, then you include leprechauns on your personal list of objective realities; their existence, in your view, is an objective fact.

Failure to draw a conceptual distinction can have dire consequences for your thinking. As we've seen, there is a clear distinction between what is the case and what I (or you, or anybody, including an entire society) believe to be the case. If you reject this conceptual distinction, you must also reject the distinction between correct and incorrect beliefs, between true and false beliefs, and between accurate and inaccurate accounts of the world. If no one's beliefs are true, then no one's beliefs are false. At any rate, if you reject these distinctions, it is hard to see how you can consistently think that anyone else should care about what you have to say about anything. In a real sense, from your perspective, you have nothing to tell the rest of us.

Some conceptual distinctions have proved so useful when philosophizing that it is very likely you will encounter them if you dip into contemporary philosophical literature. Here is a list of some of the most common distinctions:

1. *A priori/a posteriori.* *A priori* means "prior to or independent of experience," which is contrasted with the *a posteriori* or empirical. The terms are used to mark a distinction between, for example, kinds of propositions and kinds of knowledge. A true a priori proposition, such as "No square is a circle," does not depend for its truth on how things are in the world—that is, on empirical reality; the truth of an a posteriori proposition, such as "Princess Diana died before her son was crowned king," does. A priori knowledge, unlike a posteriori or empirical knowledge, does not derive at all from experience.

2. *Analytic/synthetic.* These terms are used to mark a contrast between two kinds of statements, propositions, or judgments. The truth of an analytic statement—for example, "A bachelor is an unmarried male"—deduc-

tively follows from definitions. Synthetic statements, such as "There are no bachelors in Denver," are neither true nor false merely in virtue of definitions.

3. *Contingent/necessary.* These terms pick out properties belonging to statements, states of affairs, or events. Whatever is contingent is neither impossible nor necessary—that is, both possible and non-necessary. "There are penguins in New Zealand" is a contingent statement; it is contingently (but not necessarily) true. It is not possible for a necessary statement such as "2 + 2 = 4" to be false.

4. *Type/token.* A token is an existing instance of a general type of thing or feature. For example, in the sentence "The cat is on the mat, and the mat is under the cat," there are two tokens of the word-type "cat."

5. *Descriptive/normative.* These terms are also used to mark a contrast between two kinds of statements, propositions, or judgments. A descriptive judgment is nonnormative; it merely describes the way things are without implying any judgment about whether the circumstances described are good or bad. A normative statement evaluates something as good or bad, better or worse, or as what ought or ought not to be the case. "Most Americans believe capital punishment is not wrong" is descriptive; "Capital punishment is wrong" is normative.

CHAPTER 6

Making Truth Your Aim

W<small>E HAVE SEEN THAT TO HAVE A BELIEF IS TO BELIEVE THAT WHAT</small>
you believe—that is, the proposition believed—is true. To
believe that Michael Jordan plays basketball is to believe
that it is true that Michael Jordan plays basketball. This
belief, like all of our beliefs, by nature aims at truth.
Therefore, if a belief is false, it hasn't lived up to its bill-
ing. In this way, it is like a "photograph" of you that is so
out of focus that even your mother cannot recognize the
subject. Such a photograph is still a photograph, and a
false belief is still a belief, but neither serves the point of
having it.

These considerations suggest the most basic goal for
managing your belief system: *Seek to hold and preserve true*

beliefs and avoid forming and preserving false ones. Most people, consciously or unconsciously, accept this as an ideal for their intellectual lives. However, that's only because most of us care about the truth of our beliefs (or, at least, of some of our beliefs). But what about the person who says the following?

> "I don't really care if my beliefs are true or false. All that matters to me is that they work for me. They're my beliefs and that's enough for me. I think they're true and I don't really care what other people think."

How should one respond to such a person?

Well, it is hard to see why someone should care that his beliefs are true unless a case can be made that it is important "to get it right." But is it? The answer depends partly on which beliefs we're talking about. It's clear that it really is not very important whether some of our beliefs are true. For example, I believe that UCLA has a larger student body than Harvard, that there are no snakes in Ireland, and that the largest moth in the world is the hercules moth of Papua New Guinea. However, although I might be mildly surprised to learn that these beliefs of mine are false, it would not really affect my life; I would not care very much if I'm mistaken. Suppose someone told you that your belief that you can buy potato chips at your local grocery store today is false. In the absence of some bizarre pathological need to buy potato chips today, wouldn't the proper response be "So what?"?

But sometimes what you believe really does matter. When I was a freshman in college, the nation had a scarcity of electrical engineers. For this reason, a lot of science students were advised to take electrical engineering as a major. These students believed that a good job was waiting for them upon graduation. Unfortunately, by the time they graduated there was a nationwide glut of electrical engineers, and many of them had to find another way to make a living. The truth of their belief mattered strongly for most of them.

Years ago my brother was working for a large oil-drilling company in Oklahoma. His job was to drive to oil rigs in the central states and repair electrical equipment. At the time he had just purchased a new camera and was enthusiastic about photography. One summer evening he was driving along a highway in Kansas miles away from any town, farm, or other human habitation. There was a beautiful sunset, which he decided to photograph. So he parked his pickup truck, grabbed his camera, and walked through waist-high grass into a ravine to a point where he thought he could get the best shot. He stood there taking photos for several minutes. Then he turned to go back to his truck but stopped after taking only one step, because he heard the telltale rattling of a large rattlesnake. This would have been bad enough, had several other snakes not chimed in with the chorus. There was rattling to his left, rattling to his right, rattling in front of and behind him. He decided to stop and think. After several adrenaline-enhanced moments, he decided that his options were to stand there all night or walk out. And he believed that, if he walked slowly, the rattlesnakes would probably not bite him. He was apparently right, for he lived to tell the story. It certainly mattered to him that his belief about the probability of the snakes biting him was correct when he acted on it.

We often care about what we *do,* because we do things to get what we *want.* I once heard it suggested that, put very generally, happiness is getting what you want and having happen what you want to happen. But much of what happens in our lives happens because of what we do, for human beings are not just believing beings—we are also doers or agents. We perform actions that produce results in the world. Those results often have long-range consequences. (For example, you wouldn't be here if persons thousands of years ago had not done what they did to produce their child, your distant ancestor.)

Actions are what you do. We can always ask, "Why did you do it?" If you had asked the electrical engineering majors mentioned earlier why they majored in electrical engineering, they would have said something like, "I wanted to get a good job when I graduated, and I believed that majoring in my field would make that likely." If I ask you why you exercise, you will probably tell me that you want health and long life and that you think exercise is a means to them. If you ask why I put gas in my car, then I will tell you that I want to drive my car and I believe that putting gas in it is required for it to operate.

These examples show that many of our voluntary actions are explained, at least in large part, in terms of two key factors: our desires and our beliefs. Insofar as we care about satisfying the desires underlying our actions, we should also care about the beliefs that spur us to do what we do. If these beliefs are false, then we probably will not achieve what we are aiming for. For example, if I marry Sally because I want wealth and I believe Sally is rich, then I'll be rather disappointed if, contrary to what I thought I had reason to believe, Sally is penniless. If I take a pill because I have a headache and believe that the pill is an aspirin that will merely stop the ache, then my desire will not be satisfied if the pill is really cyanide. If you want to see a movie that you believe is showing at the Fox Theater, your desire won't be satisfied when you arrive at the theater and discover that the movie isn't showing there at all.

None of this shows that you ought to care about the satisfaction of your desires. However, if you do care (and what serious person doesn't?), then this gives you a good reason also to care about the truth of your beliefs.

It is also worth pointing out that what we desire cannot be completely cut off from what we believe, because desires are often associated with beliefs. My desire to raft down the Chattahoochee River is inextricably bound up with my belief that there is such a river and such a means of navigating it. Someone's desire to graduate from college involves her belief that there is such an institution from which one can graduate. The desire of Christians or Moslems to go to heaven involves the belief that they can exist after death. If these beliefs are false, the associated desires will not have a chance of being satisfied.

Of course, it is also sometimes the case that people get a benefit from believing what is false. For example, some people obviously enjoy believing that they (or their social group) are better than the rest of us, and this belief may well allow them to mistreat others without the unpleasantness of feeling guilty. And it is possible to deceive oneself about one's own character or activities because an accurate picture would be too difficult to bear. Apparently, many executives of large tobacco companies at least still say they believe what the rest of us know is false—that their profits and livelihood are sullied by the unnecessary suffering and deaths of millions. There is usually a payoff of human self-deceit and wishful thinking.

Nevertheless, the general point still holds much if not most of the time. False beliefs, when combined with desires, can have natural consequences that most people care about avoiding. This gives us one more reason to care about avoiding false beliefs as a matter of principle.

Life-Orienting Beliefs

As I have already noted, it is a trivial matter that some beliefs we hold are false, because this falsity has little bearing on us and our lives. But there is a category of beliefs that are especially important to anyone who takes the overall direction, shape, and value of their life seriously. It makes no sense to say about the truth of such beliefs, "It doesn't matter." For it obviously does matter to the kind of person you are and the kind of life you lead. I call these beliefs "life-orienting beliefs," because holding them has a dramatic effect on the shape of your life as a whole, not only in what you *do* but in what you think you *ought* to do.

A life-orienting belief is the kind of belief that, were you to hold it throughout your life and then at the age of eighty decide that the belief is false, would lead you to completely reinterpret the shape and value of the life you had led. It is the kind of belief that systematically underlies a wide range of your thoughts and actions throughout the time you hold it. For example, suppose you spend your whole life as a devout minister or rabbi and at the age of eighty decide that your belief that God exists is false. Or suppose you decide at eighty that God exists after all, although you've always believed otherwise. In either case, this would probably lead you to drastically reevaluate your entire past life in a less favorable light. Or suppose you believed all your life that true happiness consists in the accumulation of abundant wealth and impressive social status, and you had worked hard to achieve these. If, at the age of eighty, you decide that true happiness consists in loving and helping others (something you hadn't much time for in your single-minded pursuit of fame and fortune), you will probably think your life has been deeply flawed. You might even decide, from your new perspective at eighty, that your life was a total "waste."

I hope these examples give you a good feel for what I mean by a life-orienting belief. Once you understand the idea, you can see that it is impossible to direct and shape your life without tacit or explicit appeal to some life-orienting belief or other. Either reflectively or nonreflectively, you must answer the question "In what does the Good Life consist?" Your answer to this question will provide a life-orienting belief (or set of beliefs) that will be a target at which to aim in your thoughts and actions throughout your life. It is hard to understand how any serious, responsible person could be indifferent to the truth or falsity of such beliefs. An adult who did not care would either be mentally ill or a fool.

Taking Your Worldview Seriously

You probably have realized already that intrinsically philosophical questions arise in seeking the answer to the question "What is the Good Life?" Your answer is going to depend on how you answer the metaphysical questions "What kinds of things are there?" and "How do human beings fit into the nature of things?" Here are two very different answers:

1. There is only the physical universe that science studies. Human beings are complex physical objects, like toads and trees, that cease to exist at death. There is no purpose for their existing over and above the subjective purposes each invents for his or her own life.
2. There is an omniscient, omnipotent, perfectly good God, and there is everything else, including the physical universe, which was created by God. Human beings, who survive the death of their bodies, were made to love and worship God forever.

My point is not that one of these familiar answers must be correct. (A Buddhist would say that both are false.) Rather, my point is that such answers must loom very large on the mental landscape of anyone who holds them, casting deep and long shadows on everything they think about how they should live.

Responses 1 and 2 constitute the core claims of two incompatible "worldviews" about reality. Response 1 expresses the beliefs central to philosophical naturalism, and response 2 expresses the central beliefs of classical theism. And in addition to their life-orienting nature, I want to call your attention to two further features of such accounts. First, because the sense of "world" intended in the term *worldview* is "all of reality," worldviews are *comprehensive*. Such accounts are taken by their adherents to answer the question "What is there, really?" In other words, a worldview provides a general description of all there is, and only what there is. Second, a worldview is *unsurpassable* insofar as it provides "the last word" on reality, the best deep-down account of things as they really are. If an account seems unsurpassable to me, then I believe (1) that the account cannot be replaced by or subsumed in a better account of the objects described and explained by it, and (2) that the essential features of the account will not be changed, surpassed, or superseded. And this is precisely the attitude toward a worldview taken by those who reflectively adhere to it. The importance of unsurpassability as a feature of worldviews is that it points up the fact that believing a worldview involves an intellectual commitment of a nonnegotiable kind. This commitment, when coupled with comprehensiveness, usually enters so deeply into the life, actions, and thinking of those who knowingly endorse a worldview that the abandonment of its essential features—that is, the beliefs that comprise its core account—is for them scarcely conceivable, and if conceivable certainly not desirable.

To abandon the essential features of a life-orienting worldview is to change one's mind about the necessary conditions of a life lived well. Insofar as I regard my past actions and the life I have chosen to live to be satisfactory and worthwhile, I have a big stake in the correctness of the worldview that has provided the metaphysical backdrop for my choices and behavior. And the longer one self-consciously holds a specific worldview, the greater one's stake in its being correct. This probably explains why changing one's worldview, or adopting a hitherto rejected or unknown worldview, is much more common before the age of, say, twenty-five or thirty than among people over fifty.

You may wonder why I have made this brief excursion into the nature of worldviews. Well, besides being relevant to such worldviews as classical theism and philosophical naturalism, it also allows me now to give you a different twist on what philosophizing is all about. If you want a single "big" personal aim of the activity of philosophizing, you now are in a position to understand the prime contender. There is much to be said for the view that the aim of philosophizing is to articulate, defend, and justify a worldview. This aim fits nicely with the idea that, ultimately, all philosophizing is spurred by the universal human desire to "make sense of it all."

To the prior considerations may be added one further reason why each of us should desire true life-orienting beliefs. Imagine that I have a wildly distorted view of myself and believe that I am the best basketball player in the world. When I look in the mirror I think to myself, "Ah, the best basketball player in the world is wearing a green tie today." And suppose I don't know that I am just a mediocre basketball player and that the best basketball player in the world plays in the NBA and has never worn a green tie. An enormous logical distance spans between my beliefs about myself and who I really am. The familiar phrase "to be out of touch with oneself" expresses my predicament well. In the imagined circumstances, I fail to be in touch with myself.

But now suppose that I deeply believe response 1 although response 2 is true or, alternatively, I deeply believe 2 although 1 is true. Wouldn't it be appropriate to say that in both cases I have failed to be in touch with myself, that there is a yawning chasm between my beliefs about myself and who and what I really am? If theism is false and yet I live my life consciously in light of what I believe is God's will, then surely I am out of touch with myself. Or, if philosophical naturalism is false and I live my life consciously assuming that there is no meaning or purpose to my existence over and above whatever subjective meaning or purpose I invent for it, then surely I am out of touch with myself. And most of us think it's a bad thing to be detached from oneself in this way.

We have arrived at the following conclusions. First, if you care about the shape and direction of your life, then you ought also to care about the truth of your life-orienting beliefs. Second, if you care about being in touch with yourself, then again you ought to care about the truth of your life-orienting beliefs. Third, if you care about success in your actions, then you should care about the truth of many other beliefs. Therefore, we may suppose that everyone has reason to follow the basic rule of managing their belief system: *Seek to hold and preserve true beliefs, and avoid forming and preserving false ones.*

C H A P T E R   7

Living Up to Your Own Intellectual Standards

WE SAW IN THE LAST CHAPTER THAT THE SERIOUS PERSON HAS AN interest in having true beliefs and considered a basic rule for the management of your belief system: *Seek to hold and preserve true beliefs, and avoid forming and preserving false ones.*

Unfortunately, this rule does not seem to be very helpful if what you are looking for is a recipe or algorithm to sort through your beliefs and separate the epistemic goats from the epistemic sheep. (*Epistemic,* an adjective that derives from the Greek word for "knowledge," is used to talk about matters related to belief, including justification, rationality, and knowledge.) This epistemic rule is rather like the practical advice "Do the right thing and avoid the wrong thing," which does not tell you how, exactly, to distinguish wrong actions from right actions. Moreover, the truth of our beliefs (with rare exception) is not up to us. When we "decide," for example, that Hawaii has no indigenous snakes, we don't make it true—we merely come to believe what was true all along. Because we can hardly "manage" what we have no capacity to control, the "management" of our beliefs must have to do with which beliefs we have, and not with their truth.

Furthermore, the rule really is not one rule but two: *Seek to hold and preserve true beliefs* and *Avoid forming and preserving false beliefs.* And the rule does not instruct us on which of these constituent rules is more important. Should I avoid error at all costs? I could do this by suspending belief in every proposition I entertain—by having no beliefs at all. But that doesn't seem to be what a responsible person would do and anyway would leave one with no mental map at all with which to get on in life. On the other hand, if I simply want to have the greatest number of true beliefs and don't care about the number of false beliefs I have, then I ought to believe readily and without hesitation whatever I read, hear, or consider (no matter where I read it or whom I hear it from). But that seems just crazy, especially when I think about the tabloid headlines one regularly sees while waiting in the check-out line at the grocery store. Or should I perhaps manage my belief system to maximize the *proportion* of true beliefs over false beliefs? What is clear is that following the rule will produce different belief systems depending on how such questions as these are answered.

Belief Policies

It would be easy to have true beliefs and avoid error if we had a method that would guarantee the truth of beliefs generated by its use. For example, suppose that you were constructed such that whenever you entertained a true proposition, a loud ringing in your ears results. If you considered a false proposition, the ringing is absent. And suppose you habitually trusted this ringing in your ears as a reliable truth indicator. Then you would have a sure-fire way to guarantee the truth of any proposition you already believe and any new proposition you are considering for belief. Or suppose an enormous computer database contained a real-time updated list of all and only true propositions. In that case, you could merely check any proposition against the list to find out whether it is true.

Unfortunately, we don't have such methods for guaranteeing the truth of our beliefs. But even if we did, there is an important philosophical point to be gleaned from their imagined existence. In trusting either of the proposed methods, you would be taking for granted a principle for the management of your belief system. Here are the relevant epistemic principles:

> (P1) I ought to believe that a proposition is true just in case I hear a ringing in my ears whenever I think about whether the proposition is true.

> (P2) I ought to believe that any proposition on the database list is true.

Unless you consciously or unconsciously accept such principles, even a truth-guaranteeing method of managing your beliefs will not be of any use to you.

Such principles provide standards for the management of your belief system. They tell you what beliefs you ought and ought not to hold. They also make clear what kinds of reasons or evidence entitles you to hold a particular belief. They characterize reasons for belief in the way that moral principles (for example, "You ought not to kill innocent persons") characterize reasons for actions. Because such standards are required even if you have a truth-guaranteeing method of adopting beliefs, it makes sense that they will be required for any method of adopting beliefs you rely on. In the absence of such standards, there is no way to follow the basic rule of having true beliefs and avoiding false beliefs.

Such epistemic standards or "belief policies" are unavoidable, even though their acceptance is usually tacit rather than explicit. These policies provide each person with a standard of what is to count as an adequate or sufficient reason for belief. Here are some examples of belief policies (these are only examples; I am not here endorsing any of them as correct):

- One should always proportion one's belief about a factual matter to the strength of the evidence available in support of it.
- I will believe, in matters to do with physics, all and only those claims said by holders of Nobel Prizes in that discipline to express truths.
- If you find yourself with a belief, and after reflection and investigation cannot find what seems to you any good reason for the falsity of your belief, it is OK to continue to hold that belief.
- In the absence of any overriding reasons to the contrary, I should believe whatever the Church teaches.

Your options with a belief are similar to your options with a coat: You can acquire a new one while keeping the old one, you can keep the one you have and not get a new one, or you can discard the belief you have and get a new one. Your belief policies tell you about the value and significance of evidence and thereby put constraints on acquiring, retaining, and discarding beliefs. What entitles you to believe (on the evidence you possess, and to the degree that you do) is a matter of policy. For example, if you believe, to a mild degree, what you read on the front page of the *New York Times,* you are giving tacit assent to a belief policy that indicates that seeing something written there is good evidence on the basis of which it's OK to believe what you read.

We're now in a position to consider a question that may have already occurred to you. How can we manage our beliefs unless we have control over our beliefs—that is, unless we can choose to *believe* this instead of that in the way we can sometimes choose to *do* this instead of that? This is a serious question, for it is obvious that our beliefs are not under our direct voluntary control. I cannot, for example, believe that the U.S. president is an alien *just like that* in the way that I can, just like that, snap my fingers or draw a square. Try believing (not just imagining) that the world popped into existence only five minutes ago or that all of your friends and family members are robots. You can't, however much you try.

This might lead you, as it has many philosophers, to think that choice has nothing to do with what we believe. But this would be a mistake. Breaking the smoking habit, for example, can be a matter of choice even though a person cannot break the habit just like that. This is where belief policies come in. As with the action policies we adopt to govern what we do, we can often choose which belief policies to adopt or retain in managing our beliefs. And since belief policies themselves determine what is to count as evidence, how we choose depends on a wide range of nonevidential considerations. For instance, if I fear error to an extreme degree, I may adopt the following belief policy: *I will only believe what I think is absolutely certain.* But a person who thinks that true success in life depends on taking significant risks, including risks about truth, might hold a different belief policy, such as *I will believe whatever I think is possibly true on the available evidence and whose falsity is not beyond doubt.* Following a belief policy is an intellectual habit. You may not be able to change your beliefs directly, but you can sometimes choose to change your intellectual habits, and over time this choice will repercuss throughout your set of beliefs.

To summarize: Our belief policies provide us with the intellectual standards for acquiring, retaining, or discarding our beliefs. We cannot avoid commitment to such belief policies if we want to be rational about our beliefs, for these policies set the standards for reasonableness or rationality.

Subjective Rationality

Because it is common when philosophizing to ask whether a philosophical view is rational, it behooves us to think a bit more about the notion of rationality. Before addressing this topic directly, however, I have another story to tell. Suppose a Chinese man from a remote village in a rural province of China has been imprisoned by his political enemies in a room with no windows and two closed doors. His captors inform him (1) no food or drink will be brought to him, (2) each door is unlocked, and (3) nourishment is behind only one of the doors. However, the doors have been electronically rigged in the following way: As soon as one of the doors is opened even slightly, it will continue to open automatically, while the other door will be simultaneously and permanently locked. The man reads a little Chinese, but no English. Over one of the doors in large, legible letters is scrawled "FOOD," over the other door "TIGER." These symbols mean no more to him linguistically than Chinese writing means to the average American. But, after a day or so without anything to eat or drink, it occurs to him that he once saw the inscription "TIGER" on a tin of canned meat he purchased at the village store. So he thinks that he has had an intellectual breakthrough, and he starts to believe that this must be the door behind which he will satisfy his hunger and thirst.

Given his goal of escaping his prison and getting food and drink, what is the rational thing for the man to believe and do? Well, the answer to this question depends entirely on the *perspective* we adopt. If we project ourselves into the prisoner's intellectual shoes and look at his dilemma from his perspective, then we may be willing to concede, first, that it is reasonable for him to believe that he has found the food door and, second, that it is reasonable for him to open that door (and, unfortunately, meet his doom). Given his beliefs and the resources available to him, his choice to open the "TIGER" door is not at all unreasonable. However, although from his perspective it may be reasonable for him to believe that "TIGER" means "food," we don't think he has good reason to open the "TIGER" door, since we are privy to facts of which he is unaware.

As this story shows, we are sometimes interested in evaluating someone else's beliefs from that person's own subjective perspective. We want to know whether she has lived up to her own standards. And we may judge that someone's belief is "rational" for her even though we think the belief is mistaken, and even though in fact we think there are no objectively good reasons for the truth of her belief. Let's call this sense of rationality "subjective rationality."

We can now use the idea of a belief policy to characterize subjective rationality. *A belief is subjectively rational for person A if it is in accordance with A's belief policies. Otherwise, it is subjectively irrational for A.* To hold subjectively rational beliefs is to live up to your own intellectual standards, which is what we would expect a responsible person to do. Notice that this makes the subjective rationality of a belief (but not the belief's truth) unavoidably person-relative, first, because people have different beliefs and, second, because people are going to disagree about which belief policies are correct, just as people disagree over the correctness of various action-guiding policies.

Of course, we can argue about the correctness of belief policies and sometimes change our minds. For example, many people when they were children gave tacit assent to the following belief policy: *I will believe anything I read in the newspaper.* But most adults would argue that this is not a good policy for managing your beliefs. What you don't want to be, as a serious and responsible person, is out of step with your own belief policies, for then you may be aptly criticized for flouting the very intellectual standards that you have adopted for yourself.

There is an analogy here with action policies. Suppose you accept the following action policy: *I will not drink alcoholic beverages.* Because I don't accept this policy,

I can't be criticized in the same way that you can for drinking a martini. Likewise, if you hold the belief policy *One should only believe what is empirically testable,* then you may be criticized for believing such propositions as "The rape and murder of children is wrong" and "It is better to be a successful attorney than a drug addict."

Beliefs subjectively rational for you are beliefs it is epistemically OK for you to hold. Insofar as we are interested in living up to our own intellectual standards, we are interested in having subjectively rational beliefs. (Of course, we also each hope that our subjectively rational beliefs are true.) Insofar as your beliefs are subjectively rational, you will not have failed to believe what you should have believed or have believed what you should not have believed (assuming, of course, your beliefs and belief policies). Subjective rationality requires that we have beliefs that are to our own intellectual satisfaction (but not necessarily to everybody else's).

This doesn't mean that "anything goes" just so long as you are satisfied with your own beliefs. Just because you think that you have lived up to your intellectual standards doesn't mean that you really have, any more than thinking that you haven't wronged someone means that you have not. Just as someone else may be able to see that you are being a moral hypocrite even though you don't realize it, someone else may be able to "call you on the carpet" for not living up to your intellectual standards. So, as does doing the right thing morally, doing the right thing intellectually often requires reflection, self-knowledge, and effort on everyone's part.

Objective Rationality

You may have realized that this subjective notion of rationality is incomplete. When I ask whether someone's belief is subjectively rational, I want to answer the question "What would it be rational for someone else to believe, given their belief policies and circumstances?" If I decide that, from that person's perspective, it is rational to believe that the Earth is flat, this doesn't commit me to belief in a flat Earth. To say a belief is subjectively "rational" on someone else's beliefs and belief policies is not to say there really are good reasons to adopt that belief. It is merely to say that there *appear to be* such reasons to some person. But I can't play this game if I am deliberating about what it is rational for me to believe, for I'm not merely deliberating about *my* standards. I am deliberating—to be sure, from my perspective—about the *objectively* correct standards. I am deliberating about what is *objectively* rational to believe true or likely true.

First-person, present-tense ascriptions of reasons (ascriptions I make now, such as "It is rational to believe God exists" or "It is rational to believe the earth is over 10,000 years old") are thus objective. This point may seem odd at first, since it is natural to think of first-person ("I"), present-tense ("now") concerns as subjective and historically limited. But it's not odd once you recognize the distinction between *reporting* reasons and *endorsing* reasons. It's easy for me to imagine contexts in which I project myself into your subjective perspective and agree that, from your perspective, you have adequate reasons to believe some proposition even though I don't endorse those reasons, because I don't think they're objectively adequate. For example, suppose you've had a dramatic religious experience in which you took God to be talking to you, and this experience is one of your reasons for believing that God exists. Even if I were an atheist, I could agree that, from your perspective, this experience provides you with an adequate reason for your belief. But this judgment will have no tendency to make me believe. I can *report* your reasons without *endorsing* those reasons.

However, this distinction between reporting and endorsing reasons collapses in the first-person. If I judge myself to have reasons to believe such and such, I ordinarily cannot withhold endorsement of those reasons. I cannot add the qualification that these reasons are not objectively adequate, that they merely appear so from my perspective.

Suppose you and I go on a backpacking trip in the Appalachian mountains, and suppose it is a region I have never visited before, having lived in Manhattan all my life. You are an avid amateur naturalist. I am an urban cowboy who doesn't know the difference between a toad and a frog. As we are hiking along the Appalachian Trail one sunny summer day, I notice a serpentine figure beside the path, and I ask you, "Are there any good reasons to believe that this snake is poisonous?" It would be a joke if you replied, "Well, *you* might well be rational if you think so. I can imagine that, from your perspective, it's OK to believe that's a poisonous snake." This would be a joke, because it's *really* good reasons I'm interested in, not just *apparently* good ones. But note that my question is equivalent to "Are there any good reasons *for me* to believe this snake is poisonous?"

Selecting Belief Policies

How do we decide which belief policies to use in managing our belief systems? One method would be to suspend judgment on the truth of all of our beliefs and go searching for a "method" or belief policy whose use will guarantee true (or probably true) beliefs. The idea is to throw all of the epistemic apples out of the barrel and only put the ones not rotten back in. But this approach (one made famous by Descartes) seems doomed to failure. In the absence of any propositions believed true, the choice of a satisfactory belief policy will be purely arbitrary.

For example, suppose you say you're going to doubt the truth of all your beliefs and only let back into your belief system those beliefs that science has established. This approach only makes sense if you assume that the beliefs established by science are true, which means that you haven't really called *those* beliefs in question at all.

You've made an exception of scientific beliefs, and then concluded (not surprisingly) that the following is a truth-engendering belief policy: *It's OK to believe whatever I take to be a truth established by scientific investigation.* (Another difficulty: How will you tell whether a belief *has* been "established" by science? You will need criteria for distinguishing what really has been established by science from what has not, and you could not find—and certainly could not justify—such criteria without prior belief about the "findings" of science.)

A better approach is to begin with your initial stock of beliefs—that is, to assume that you do indeed have lots of true or likely true beliefs—and seek to discover and clarify belief policies that underlie the reasonableness of these beliefs. You can then use these belief policies in managing your belief system. This doesn't mean that you cannot sometimes decide to reject a belief policy you realize you hold or have held. What it does mean is that, with respect to your goal of having true or likely true beliefs, your belief policies are "innocent until proven guilty" of leading you to false beliefs.

For example, suppose you find yourself with the belief that Hitler was wicked and the belief that apartheid is wrong. And suppose you realize that you endorse the following belief policy: *I will only believe what is testable solely by observation.* If you hold this policy, you will have to discard your beliefs about Hitler and apartheid. In so far as you consider these beliefs true, you will want to reject any belief policy that prohibits your holding them.

CHAPTER 8

Arguments

Philosophizing is the enterprise of reasoning about philosophical issues. As you already know, such reasoning will involve the construction and evaluation of arguments. Therefore, if you are going to philosophize well, you need to develop your intellectual skills to the degree that you can at least spot a good or bad argument when you meet one.

The premises of an argument are intended to provide a reason to believe the conclusion. Good arguments differ depending on the degree of support that the premises confer on the conclusion. A good *deductive* argument provides a conclusive reason to believe that its conclusion is true. A good *inductive* argument provides some reason—perhaps even a very strong reason—but not a conclusive reason to believe its conclusion.

Deductive Arguments

One way to begin to get a handle on the nature of good deductive arguments is to look at some bad ones. Here, for example, is an argument you won't be tempted to embrace:

1. My grandmother was born in Birmingham. Therefore, the physical universe began with an enormous explosion.

The problem with this argument is not that the only premise is false (take my word for it; it is true) or that the conclusion is false (it also is true, according to current science). The problem has to do with the connection between the premise and the conclusion it is supposed to support. Even if the premise is true, it just isn't a reason to believe that the conclusion is true. That my grandmother was born in Birmingham has nothing to do with the way the universe began. In other words, the conclusion "does not follow" from the premise.

This flaw is not shared by the following argument:

2. Paul McCartney is a kangaroo. All kangaroos are marsupials. Hence, Paul McCartney is a marsupial.

In this argument the premises provide a conclusive reason to believe the conclusion. Whatever is wrong with argument 2, it's not what is wrong with argument 1. The conclusion of argument 2 must be true if the premises are true.

Argument 2, unlike argument 1, is what logicians call a "valid" argument. A valid argument has the following property: *If its premises are true, its conclusion must be true.* Note that the premises of a valid argument need not *in fact* be true. Argument 2 is valid even though it has a false premise; Paul McCartney is not a kangaroo. Argument 1 is an invalid argument.

When philosophizing, the first question you want to ask of any deductive argument is "Is it valid?" If it is not, then the premises cannot give you or anyone else a conclusive reason to believe the conclusion. If it is, you can proceed to the next question: "Are the premises true?"

Philosophers are understandably delighted when they can discover valid deductive arguments, with premises they believe, for a view they wish to propound. This is the stuff "knock-down" arguments for or against philosophical views are made of. Consider the following well-known argument against determinism, the view that, at any moment of time, there is only one possible future course of events:

> If determinism is true, then there are no free actions.
> There are free actions.
> Therefore, determinism is false.

Or consider the following argument against physicalism, the view that everything that exists is physical:

> If there are psychological facts, then physicalism is false.
> There are psychological facts.
> Therefore, physicalism is false.

My point here is not that either of these arguments really does provide a conclusive reason for its conclusions. Some philosophers think the premises are true; others don't. But the arguments are clearly valid, and so *if* their premises are true, the truth of their conclusions is necessitated.

Reductio Arguments

If you begin to read philosophical literature, you will quickly come across a kind of knock-down deductive argument that goes by the impressive Latin name *reductio ad absurdum*. A "reductio" argument demonstrates how absurd—that is, obviously false—claims follow logically from some philosophical view. The strategy is to suppose that the view is true and see what follows. If it can be shown that absurd results follow, this provides one with conclusive grounds to reject the view.

To illustrate how this works, consider the familiar idea of a time machine found in popular fiction and movies. A time machine is a device you can get into and "travel" to some physical place in the distant past (for example, to the inauguration ceremony of Julius Caesar) or in the distant future (for example, to year 3000). When you get "there," you essentially plug into the same physical network of causes and effects that every other human being has. You take up physical space, you eat, you see and are seen by other people, you talk to and are heard by others, you make footprints in the sand, you cast shadows in the noonday sun, and so on. You're just another human being in the world, except you're a "visitor" from another time.

Is such a machine possible? Could you build a machine that allowed you to travel through time in the way described? Well, you'll have to decide for yourself. Here's one reductio against the view that H. G. Wells–style time travel is possible. Suppose you had such a machine at your disposal. Then it follows that the following claim must be true: (P) *You can bring it about that you were never born.* Very easily, indeed. All you have to do is travel to the time and place where one of your parents is five years old and kill him or her. But this isn't possible, for "you" are the person who was born a specific number of years before stepping into the time machine. P can't be true, because it generates a contradiction. It says that the person who steps into the time machine can bring it about that he or she was never born and so never stepped into the time machine (and so can't bring anything about by using a time machine). I'll leave it to you to find other contradictory claims that follow from the idea of a time machine.

Inductive Arguments

A great many good arguments we accept in science and daily life don't provide us with the sort of strong reason for belief supplied by deductive arguments. For example:

All observed crows are scavengers.
X is a crow.
Therefore, X is a scavenger.

Most persons living in France speak French.
Michelle lives in France.
Therefore, Michelle speaks French.

Rats who smoke the rat equivalent of three packs of cigarettes per day display a higher incidence of lung cancer.
Rats, with respect to their respiratory systems, are similar to human beings.
Therefore, humans who smoke three packs of cigarettes per day will display a higher incidence of cancer.

The Chicago Bulls usually beat their opponents in the playoffs.
The Bulls are playing tonight in the playoffs.
Therefore, the Bulls will win tonight.

I bought 900 of the tickets of a 1,000-ticket lottery.
Therefore, I will win the lottery.

If you believe their premises, each of these arguments provides you with a reason to believe the conclusion.

However, unlike the case of valid deductive arguments, it is possible for the conclusions of these inductive arguments to be false even though the premises are all true. Michelle may be that rare person who lives in France but doesn't speak French. It doesn't follow that the Bulls must win a playoff game just because they usually do. I may lose the lottery even though I have most of the tickets. None of these arguments is deductively valid. If their premises are true, they certainly give you a reason to believe in the probable truth of their conclusions. But *probable* truth is not *guaranteed* truth. And this is what distinguishes good inductive arguments from valid deductive ones.

Inductive arguments for controversial philosophical views are a commonplace. Let me give you two examples. Many scientifically inclined philosophers this century have been attracted to the view that science can explain all the facts about what there is in the physical universe. Call this view "scientism." A familiar inductive argument for scientism runs as follows. In the past, science has had enormous success in explaining a wide range of diverse facts about the physical universe, from chemical behavior to biological diversity to the origin of subatomic particles, and so on. Therefore, runs the argument, this provides strong evidence to believe that, for any currently inexplicable physical facts, a scientific explanation will eventually be found. There is no fact about the world that science won't eventually be able to explain. Proponents of this inductive argument recognize that the truth of scientism isn't *entailed* by the past success of science in explaining so many different kinds of physical facts. But they think the past success of science does give you some reason to accept scientism.

Now for my second example. A contemporary version of the argument from design for the existence of God has focused on the exquisite fine-tuning of the laws or regularities of nature. In the last thirty years there has been a vast expansion of scientific knowledge concerning the origins of the universe and of life on Earth. It turns out that the fundamental constants of physics—the gravitational force, the strength of the weak and strong nuclear forces, the speed of light—must have values that fall within an extremely narrow range for life to be so much as possible. If there had been even minute deviations in any one of them (for example, if the gravitational constant had been different even to a minuscule degree), stars and habitable planets could not have developed and life (at least chemistry-based life, the only kind we know of) would have been impossible. It would be astonishing, runs the argument, if such a vast array of life-facilitating coincidences have come about by chance. This makes plausible the thought that the world was designed or created by an intelligent Designer who intended the existence of living things and eventually rational, intelligent, morally significant creatures. Again, proponents of this argument don't think that the conclusion *follows* by necessity from the premises but that the premises do give you a good reason to accept the conclusion.

In practice, philosophical arguments you encounter will often involve both deductive and inductive elements. Some of the premises of a deductive argument may themselves be supported by inductive reasoning. The premises of an inductive argument may include claims supported by deductive reasoning.

Using Inductive and Deductive Arguments

How does all of this relate to our earlier discussion of belief policies and rationality? Well, first consider deductive arguments. It might seem plausible, at least initially, that a person who accepts the general belief policy *Seek to hold and preserve true beliefs, and avoid forming and preserving false ones* will thereby have a good reason to adopt the following belief policy: *Whenever I believe that P, I ought to believe whatever propositions follow deductively from P.* For example, whenever I believe that P and also believe that Q follows from P, I ought to believe that Q. Deductive arguments provide a tool for the removal of a guaranteed falsity in your belief system and so can aid in your pursuit of a belief system that is comprehensive and accurate. Arguments can do this by exposing logical inconsistencies in your beliefs. A factual proposition ("There is life on Mars") and its denial ("It is not the case that there is life on Mars") cannot both be true in the same sense at the same time. If you believe both P and its denial not-P, then one of these beliefs must be false. There is an explicit inconsistency in your perspective.

However, it is probably rare that educated adults self-consciously hold such explicitly contradictory beliefs. It is more common that we hold beliefs that are *implicitly* inconsistent. For example, suppose I believe that whatever is real is a physical object but also that there is a lot of love in my family. My beliefs are not explicitly inconsistent, because what I believe in one case does not explicitly deny what I believe in the other. But it is easy to boil explicit inconsistency to the surface of my belief system with a simple argument:

1. Whatever is real is a physical object.
2. Love is not a physical object.
Therefore:
3. Love is not real.
Therefore:
4. There is not a lot of love in my family.

Statement 4 is the denial of my belief that there is a lot of love in my family. The argument shows that my belief that whatever is real is a physical object and my belief that there is a lot of love in my family are implicitly inconsistent, for it reveals an explicit inconsistency. To remove the inconsistency, I must give up at least one of the beliefs.

However, the valid argument doesn't tell me *which* of my beliefs I should give up. I can preserve consistency by giving up either the belief about physical objects or the belief about love. And I should warn you that this point brings to light what is commonly overlooked in contexts where philosophers are aiming to construct knock-down deductive arguments. The discovery of a valid argument provides you with a good reason to do one of two things: (1) to reject at least one of the premises (so, if you believe them all, stop it) or (2) to accept the conclusion. The discovery of the argument itself won't tell you which to do. Instead, considerations external to the argument must be consulted. Of course, if you believe that the argument's premises are beyond doubt, then maybe you should believe the conclusion. But this isn't obvious. Suppose the conclusion is bizarre or repugnant or absurd to you, although before hitting on the argument, you didn't realize that it followed from premises you always thought were indubitable. You might just decide that you've found a new reason to doubt the premises you never before thought doubtable, instead of a reason to believe the conclusion.

Philosophers often disagree over whether a particular proposition does follow from a set of premises—that is, whether a particular deductive argument really is valid. But two philosophers may well agree that an argument is valid yet disagree about what it provides a reason to believe. In short, the mere discovery of a valid argument (even one with premises you accept) doesn't settle the issue of what to believe.

The issue of free will and physical determinism provides a good example of this sort of epistemic situation. (Physical determinism is the view that at any moment of time there is only one physically possible future course of events.) Consider the following argument:

1. Physical determinism is correct.
2. If (1), then human beings never act freely.
Therefore, human beings never act freely.

This is a valid argument. But some philosophers take the argument to provide a good reason to reject human freedom, whereas others find the conclusion so crazy and absurd that they take the argument to provide the best possible reason to reject the first premise. The first camp are impressed with the inductive grounds for statement 1. The second camp believe that the conclusion is so obviously false that inductive considerations could never suffice to establish it. Such circumstances often provoke defenders of a controversial philosophical view to respond to the "knock-down" deductive reasoning of their objectors as follows: "What you state is no *objection* to my view. It's a logical *consequence* of my view." "Exactly," one can imagine the objectors responding.

In light of these considerations, the belief policy mentioned earlier (*Whenever I believe that P, I ought to believe whatever propositions follow deductively from P*) will need qualification. It should be adopted as merely a provisional guideline, for to do otherwise would require that the beliefs one has at any moment of time are sacrosanct. And, of course, if this were so, it would never be rational to quit believing what one once believed or to begin to believe what one once didn't believe.

I can't always believe what follows from P and preserve consistency in my belief system. Suppose, for example, that I now believe P and R, and discover that Q follows from P, and not-Q follows from R. What I've discovered is a good reason to eschew belief that *both* P and R, but now I have to decide *which* to believe. In other words, the above belief policy should be followed only when it doesn't conflict with a more general policy, something such as *Insofar as I am able, I will preserve consistency in my belief system.*

Things get even more complicated with inductive reasoning. The premises of a good inductive argument are supposed to provide one with support, but not conclusive support, for the truth of the conclusion. But to tell whether an inductive argument really does provide a reason for belief, we've first got to determine whether the kinds of facts described in the premises are the kind that can serve as good evidence for the conclusion. For example, consider the following argument:

All the crows ever observed have been black.
Therefore, all crows are black.

Certain conditions must be satisfied for this to be a good inductive argument. It must be the case that the sample of crows is representative. The premise will be defeated if there is reason to believe that a significant proportion of the population of all crows could not have been sampled. (For example, suppose 90 percent of all crows live outside Canada but all observations were made there.) Such conditions can be generalized into inductive standards such as "A random, representative sampling of a population of things X that finds that all sampled Xs have feature Y is good evidence for the claim that all Xs have feature Y."

Notice that such inductive standards themselves constitute belief policies that are likely to differ from person to person, especially when you consider that what is at issue, in part, is what kinds of facts provide evidence for the truth of beliefs about different subjects. Again, this doesn't mean that "anything goes" when it comes to inductive standards. We can often defend the view that someone's inductive standard is defective. For example, suppose someone tells me that they believe it is going to rain tomorrow. When I ask why they believe this, they tell me that they asked the Ouija board last night whether it was going to rain. They seem to be endorsing the following inductive standard: *What the Ouija board indicates in response to questions about the weather provides good evidence for the truth of beliefs about the weather.* The reason most of us don't think this is a plausible inductive standard is that we think it is possible to establish empirically that there is no even roughly systematic relation between what the Ouija board says and what happens meteorologically. Unlike the weather report on daily news, the Ouija board is not even a roughly reliable source of evidence for beliefs about future weather events.

Differences in inductive standards are as common as differences in opinion about the reliable sources of information. The American philosopher William James, for example, distinguished between scientific beliefs and philosophical beliefs and held that strict evidential standards applied only to the former. Moreover, even when persons agree on the kind of evidence that would provide support for a particular claim, they may disagree on whether the facts provide such evidence. This is the case when scientists in the same field, accepting the same data, nevertheless disagree about whether that data constitute adequate support for some claim. An excellent recent example is the dispute over whether a meteorite from Mars provides evidence for microbial life long ago on that planet. At the time I am writing this, scientists with seemingly identical inductive standards of evidence agree on the microscopic structures found in this meteorite but disagree on whether the structures constitute good evidence for microbial life.

Background, experience, and expertise are sometimes a source of disagreement over inductive standards. If the majority of trained evolutionary biologists believe some claim about the development of vertebrates, I and other nonexperts may take this as some reason to believe the claim. But it may not count as evidence at all for the famous Harvard paleontologist Stephen Jay Gould.

People often differ on how much evidence is required to generate a good reason for belief, and this difference will be reflected in their inductive standards. The strength of the evidence plays an especially important role in probabilistic reasoning. In many philosophical contexts, it is just assumed that the rational person will believe whatever he or she decides is more likely than not on the available evidence (that is, whatever has a probability greater than .5). So suppose, after honest, sincere investigation, I decide that I have grounds to believe that the probability of proposition P is .65—that is, quite a bit above the .5 threshold. According to the suggested inductive standard, if I want to remain a rational person, then I ought to believe that P. But what if P entails the falsity of numerous important beliefs of mine, beliefs that are stable and established and for all of which I have what I think are good, although not conclusive, reasons for believing? Suppose many of those beliefs are well-entrenched, life-orienting beliefs. Then would it really be reasonable to believe P as soon as I decide that the likelihood of P's truth well exceeds .5? I don't think so, and I'll bet most of my readers agree.

Arguments to the Best Explanation

There is another kind of argument you probably will encounter less frequently in philosophical literature but that is nonetheless important. The American philosopher C. S. Peirce called arguments of this third type "abductive" arguments, but they are more commonly referred to by the expression "inference to the best explanation."

Suppose I awake in the middle the night with a terrific pain in my chest near my heart. Recalling that my physician recently gave me a clean bill of cardiac health, that I ate a very spicy Indian curry for dinner the night before, and that such food can cause heartburn, I formulate a hypothesis: the curry caused my pain. Other hypotheses would explain the phenomenon (for example, that I am having a heart attack or that I am a victim of witchcraft). Nevertheless, if the other hypotheses are less plausible, I am entitled to adopt the "best explanation" and conclude that the spicy curry probably caused my chest pain.

The strength of arguments to the best explanation depends on the absence of equally plausible alternative hypotheses. For example, if I have other symptoms of a heart attack, the hypothesis that my chest pains are caused by a heart attack must be taken more seriously. My inference to "Spicy curry caused my chest pain" will be weakened to the degree that there is a plausible alternative hypothesis.

One advantage of arguments to the best explanation is that they make possible the construction of a cumulative case that appeals to a wide range of facts in need of explanation. For example, my belief that Australia is an island is not based on any rigorous deductive or inductive argument. If asked to defend it, I can appeal to a variety of independent considerations that support it. Like you, I was taught so in my childhood. It is so on all the maps. I've never heard it contradicted or questioned. Everyone I ever talked with about Australia, every Australian ever met, every movie I've seen set in Australia, and every television show about Australian wildlife took it for granted that Australia is an island. The most plausible explanation of this complex set of independent facts is that Australia *is* an island. Of course, in this case, no remotely plausible alternative hypothesis exists.

What Makes a Good Explanation?

There is no rigorous algorithm to determine that one hypothesis is a more plausible explanation than the alternatives. However, some general guidelines will help you in your evaluation. First, a good explanation should illuminate phenomena that you wouldn't expect to happen in the normal course of things. This merely highlights the fact that we don't usually seek explanations of facts we regard as in no way surprising. We don't tend to ask "Why?" of unsurprising phenomena. Second, a good explanation should fit with background evidence. A great many hypotheses, if true, would explain why all the lights in my house go out during a thunderstorm. Here are two: "A witch has cast a spell on my house" and "A tyrannosaurus rex has chewed through the power line leading to my neighborhood." I am not likely to take these explanations seriously, because I consider them extremely improbable on my background evidence. Third, with a good explanation, the facts in need of explaining should be much more likely to occur if the proposed explanation is true.

Suppose that a bank robbery has occurred, and you are considering whether Wilbur is guilty of the robbery. Here are the facts:

1. Wilbur's fingerprints were found on the bank's safe.
2. Wilbur has no good alibi.
3. Wilbur was recently fired from the bank that was robbed and told his boss in anger, "You'll live to regret this!"
4. A large sum of money was deposited in a Swiss bank account in Wilbur's name the week after the robbery.
5. Wilbur paid cash for a new Lexus the day after the robbery.

If this is all the evidence you have and no alternative hypothesis is forthcoming, then Wilbur's guilt may look like a pretty good—even the best—explanation. Notice how each of statements 1 through 5 individually constitutes only weak evidence, but together they generate a strong cumulative case. But suppose you learn that Wilbur's job at the bank involved opening the safe daily. Then statement 1 is no longer surprising, nor is it more likely to be true if Wilbur is guilty. And suppose that you learn that Wilbur's rich aunt died and bequeathed him a large sum of money that arrived in the form of a check the day of the robbery. In that case, statements 4 and 5 are not *more* likely to be true on the hypothesis that Wilbur is guilty. There's a perfectly plausible alternative explanation that involves Wilbur's innocence.

Cumulative case arguments are especially suited to the rational defense of philosophical hypotheses proffered as an explanation of a wide range of facts. Worldviews such as classical theism, philosophical naturalism, and Buddhism are intended to explain the widest possible range of facts—namely, *every* fact. And so it is not surprising that one can find theists, naturalists, and Buddhists arguing that their respective account provides the best explanation of such diverse facts as religious, moral, and aesthetic experience; the existence of life on Earth; human nature; the success of science; the intelligibility and orderliness of the universe; the existence of conscious, rational beings; and the widespread suffering of animals. For each of us, the important question is this: "What worldview, in light of all your experience and reflection, in light of all that you know and reasonably believe, provides the most plausible explanation of what there is?" Given the complexity and breadth of the evidence, combined with the judgment required to assess not only what are the facts but how one explanation compares with the alternatives (in each case and over all), it is not surprising that honest, sincere, intelligent persons can arrive at different conclusions.

The Sources of Belief

NOT ALL OF OUR BELIEFS CAN BE BASED ON STATEABLE REASONS that can serve as premises of an argument for what is believed. Unless it is possible to have beliefs without inferring them from something else you believe, it is not possible to have beliefs at all. Fortunately, human beings are endowed with psychological mechanisms that produce beliefs in us automatically, unless we act to short-circuit their natural effects.

Memory

If you ask me why I believe I have been to France, then I will tell you that I remember many experiences I had while visiting there as a student. If you ask me why I believe I remember, then I may tell you that I have lots of memories of France—at least, I certainly seem to remember lots of experiences there—and I know of no reason to believe that all of these apparent memories are inaccurate. You could, of course, ask me for a reason why I think my memories are genuine memories, and I could show you photographs and put you in touch with friends who could tell you that they remember being with me in France. But their testimony is only useful insofar as their memory is a reliable source of information (that is, true beliefs) about the past. If you ask me why I seem to remember, for example, seeing the Eiffel Tower, then I cannot give you a reason from which I have inferred my belief that I did: I just find myself having the appropriate memory belief whenever I direct my attention to my trip to France.

Memory is one of the psychological mechanisms that produces beliefs in human beings automatically, thereby providing us with what philosophers have called "basic" beliefs—beliefs that properly serve as ultimate starting points in our reasoning. A basic belief is a belief that it is rational to hold without holding it on the basis of any other proposition or belief at all. And we can fit the rationality of basic beliefs fairly easily into our earlier discussion of belief policies and rationality. With respect to memory, the relevant belief policy runs something like this: *In the absence of any reason to believe otherwise, you ought to believe that you remember what you think you remember.* This is a belief policy we all subscribe to in our habitual reliance on the "deliverances" of memory. And a general umbrella belief policy is going to be attached to all sources of basic belief, something like this: *In the absence of any reason to believe otherwise, you ought to continue to hold a belief generated by a source of basic beliefs.*

Memory is a source of basic beliefs, as is sense perception. These sources are generally reliable but not infallible, which is to say that a basic belief can be false. Memory *preserves* our beliefs and *enables us to call them up.*

However, our memory can preserve a false belief as well as a true one; it is possible to misremember. For example, suppose last Tuesday I thought I saw an acquaintance of mine, Barbara, from a distance at the airport. I thus now "remember" that I saw Barbara at the airport last Tuesday. But, unbeknownst to me, Barbara has an identical twin sister Mary, and it was Mary I saw. Nevertheless, in spite of their fallibility, without trusting in the general reliability of memory and these other sources of belief, our belief systems would be not merely sketchy but nonexistent. Memory plays a key role in our reasoning, for it enables us to *draw on our own beliefs to supply premises in reasoning and arguments.* For example, we solve mathematical problems using memorized theorems, and we evaluate arguments using memorized characterizations of "good" and "bad" arguments.

Perception

Perception is another source of basic beliefs. I do not infer that the mockingbird is sitting in the tree when I see the bird. I visually *perceive* the bird, which immediately produces in me the belief that the mockingbird is there. I hear (auditorily perceive) the singing of the bird; I taste (gustatorily perceive) the sweetness of the cookie; I feel (tactually perceive) the smoothness of the table top; I smell (olfactorily perceive) the baking garlic. These sensory modes give me perceptual access to the physical world around me. If you ask me why I believe the computer screen before me is illuminated, the appropriate answer is that I can just *see* that it is illuminated. From this perceptual belief I can infer, given my other beliefs, that the computer is turned on and that the electrical power in my house is not out. Like memory, perception is a fallible source of belief. I can believe that I see a log in the river when in fact the object of my visual perception is a large alligator.

Introspection

The word *introspection* derives from the Latin *introspicere,* meaning "to look within." Introspection is a capacity to attend to one's own conscious mental states and achieve a kind of inner seeing of what is going on in your mind. Most (if not all) of these "goings-on" are *experiences* (such as imagining a purple elephant or feeling a pain in your big toe or seeing a lizard) and thoughts (such as the thought of your mother's name or the thought of the sum of three and two or the thought that dead men tell no lies). You do not infer that you are in pain or that you are thinking of the amount on the last check you wrote at the bookstore. The relevant beliefs simply arise in you spontaneously through introspective awareness.

Reason

Memory, perception, and introspection provide the experiential ground of our beliefs. Let's look at how this works for a commonplace example.

Experience ⟶ **(produces)** ⟶ **Belief**

Experience	Belief
I see the elephant.	I believe the elephant is in front of me.
I look away but retain the image.	I believe I am now imaging the elephant.
I remember its shape.	I believe it has enormous ears relative to its body.

But I also believe that if the giraffe at the zoo is taller than the elephant at the zoo and the elephant is taller than the zebra, then the giraffe is taller than the zebra. On what basis do I believe this? I can certainly see that the giraffe is taller than the elephant and that the elephant is taller than the zebra. But I don't believe on the basis of perception the proposition that if the giraffe is taller than the elephant and the elephant is taller than the zebra, then the giraffe is taller than the zebra. As a rational being, I just grasp, and thereby believe, its truth. Reason is the source of my belief. As philosophers have said, the belief is "evident to reason."

Such truths are usually called "self-evident," because they are obvious in themselves: if one considers and understands them, one believes and knows them. Here are some other examples:

- If X is identical to Y and Y is identical to Z, then X is identical to Z.
- No human being is in two distant places at the same time.
- An object cannot be larger than itself.
- There are no married bachelors.

A word of caution here. You might think that *seeming* self-evident is always a guarantee that a proposition is self-evident or true. This would make reason, unlike perception, memory, and introspection, an infallible generator of beliefs—that is, a source of true beliefs only. And a strong case can be made for this view, especially if we focus on simple logical and arithmetical truths. It is, indeed, hard to see how anyone could understand the earlier principle about identity (the first example, called "the transitivity of identity") without recognizing its truth. This is supported by the fact that, were someone to deny its truth, we'd probably attribute this to a lack of understanding, which is a way of saying that his reason isn't functioning properly in this case. Nevertheless, you should be wary of thinking that, just because a proposition seems self-evident to you, it must therefore be self-evident or true.

Here's why. A generation of scientists rejected Newton's theory of gravitational forces because they took it to be self-evident that physical objects cannot act upon each other at a distance. Or consider the principle usually called "the Galilean Law of the Addition of Velocities."

This principle is a generalization, of cases such as the following:

> Suppose that an airplane is flying at a speed of 400 miles per hour relative to the ground. Suppose that inside the plane a bumblebee is flying at a speed of 25 miles per hour relative to the airplane in the direction of the plane's travel. Then, the bee's speed relative to the ground is the sum of these two speeds: 425 miles per hour.

Read over the principle again. Doesn't its truth seem to be beyond all possibility of doubt? Yet according to Einstein's Special Theory of Relativity, a theory regarded by physicists as well confirmed, useful, and correct, the Galilean Law of the Addition of Velocities is not true (although it comes extremely close to being true at the non-relativistic speeds in the example). What this example shows is that it is sometimes possible for your rational intuitions—at least when they concern *empirical* matters—to be defeated by other considerations. It doesn't show that fundamental logical principles such as the transitivity of identity may turn out to be false. And it doesn't undermine reason as a source of basic beliefs you can, and should, rely on.

Testimony

Testimony is the last source of basic beliefs we'll consider. Reliance on the word of others is an absolutely fundamental belief-generating mechanism that is pervasive in our ordinary lives. This reliance begins early on, for you would have never learned a language unless as a child you had trusted in what others told you about the *meanings* of certain sounds. You certainly were not in a position to *check* whether your mother was correct when she pointed to a tree and said "tree" or pointed to a table and said "table." In fact, most testimony is uncheckable by perceptual means, if only for the lack of time and resources. Every time you read a newspaper or textbook, or hear a newscast or weather report, and believe what you read or hear, you are trusting in the reliability of testimony as a source of true or likely true beliefs. Imagine you had to do every experiment in a physics textbook to rationally believe what you are told or had to do all the historical research to believe what you read in a book on world history. This task would be an impossible feat. Indeed, most of what we take ourselves to know about history, geography, and science is in one way or another perceptually inaccessible to us.

The importance of testimony is often overlooked when it comes to science, but the Harvard biologist Richard Lewontin makes the point so forcefully that I'll quote him here:

> Given the immense extent, inherent complexity, and counterintuitive nature of scientific knowledge, it is impossible for anyone, including non-specialist scientists, to retrace the intellectual paths that lead to scientific conclusions about nature. In the end we must trust the experts and they, in turn, exploit their authority as experts and their rhetorical skills to secure our attention and our belief in things that we do not really understand. ("Billions and Billions of Demons," *New York Review of Books* 44, no. 1 (December 1997): 28–32)

We have no choice but to trust what others tell us about a wide range of subjects. Becoming an "educated" person would be impossible without such trust.

As a source of beliefs, testimony is very like memory. In each case causal mechanisms operate in us to convey beliefs from source to recipient. Memory conveys beliefs from one's own past to one's own present. Testimony conveys beliefs from one's neighbor or interlocutor to oneself. Experience teaches each of us to override these mechanisms in special circumstances. For example, we learn to distrust memories when drunk or testimony when it comes from a source we consider unreliable (for example, a tabloid newspaper). But normally the mechanisms operate freely and automatically. Which is a good thing, for otherwise we could hardly have become the persons we are with the enormously large and complex set of beliefs each of us has.

Other Possible Sources

There may well be other sources of basic beliefs, although other candidates tend to be more controversial. Let me just mention three possibilities.

Telepathy is a psychological mechanism by which you just find yourself having information about the thoughts of someone else unmediated by normal perceptual means. I once knew an identical twin who told me that when his twin brother had been seriously injured a thousand miles away, he (the uninjured twin) knew immediately without any physical communication by phone or telegram that his brother had broken his arm. Without any apparent sensory input, he just found himself believing the truth. If there is such an ability to know things this way, then telepathy is a source of basic beliefs.

Second, many religious thinkers have held that there are other sources of knowledge besides reason, perception, memory, introspection, and testimony. For example, Aquinas, Calvin, and most representatives of the Christian tradition have held that the truths of religion are truths of *faith,* which is regarded as an additional source of basic beliefs.

Finally, consider the peculiar "sixth sense" described by the great Anglo-Indian naturalist and sportsman Jim Corbett in the book *Jungle Lore.* In the first several decades of this century, Corbett single-handedly tracked down and shot numerous man-eating leopards and tigers in the jungles of India. He said that his life was saved on numerous occasions because of an ability to be aware that an unseen and unheard dangerous cat was lurking nearby. Such an ability to sense danger without using the five normal sensory modes would have been handy to our prehistoric ancestors. If Corbett was telling the truth, he and others may have an additional source of basic beliefs.

A Final Word

We've seen that memory, perception, introspection, reason, and testimony automatically generate beliefs that are rational to hold without basing those beliefs on arguments from other beliefs. One indication that these sources are sources of *basic* beliefs is the fact that it is impossible to reclaim the beliefs derived from one source were you to lose all such beliefs along with the source itself (and be left only with the other four sources).

Suppose you lost all your memory beliefs along with your ability to remember at all. You would be in a sore epistemic predicament indeed. You would have forgotten, for example, the names of all your family and friends (not to mention your own) and such facts as that mastodons are extinct. You might be thinking, "Couldn't I recover these lost memories by someone just telling me whatever I've forgotten?" Well, no. For we're imagining that you've not only lost all your memory beliefs. This is bad enough, for it means you've forgotten the meaning and reference of all the words you once understood. After your memory loss, someone may as well say "Sha-la-la-la-boom-bang" to you as say, "Mastodons are extinct," because neither set of sounds will have the least tendency to help you acquire the lost information about mastodons. Furthermore, we're imagining you've also lost the ability to remember at all; memory itself as a source of knowledge has been wiped from your cognitive repertoire. This means you won't be able to regain the linguistic understanding that is a precondition of the belief that mastodons are extinct. Unfortunately, without memory, you won't be able to learn a language or anything else. You may, of course, continue to have fleeting, instantaneous experiences such as the taste of lemon or a twinge of pain. But, without memory, you'll have lost the next instant the awareness that you had them.

Flaws and Fallacies

SIMPLY PUT, PHILOSOPHERS TYPICALLY DO TWO THINGS WHEN THEY philosophize: They propound a philosophical view, and they defend this view at least in part by presenting arguments intended to support the view. This suggests two ways that something can go wrong with one's philosophizing. First, there can be a flaw internal to the view itself, such that the view will not bear up under critical scrutiny. In this case, merely understanding the view or what it is like for someone to hold the view will provide you with a good reason to reject it. Second, the reasoning or arguments offered in support of a philosophical view may contain errors. These mistakes usually go under the heading of "fallacies." Fallacies in reasoning are legion in kind, but the sorts of fallacies that philosophers typically accuse their peers of committing are thankfully much fewer in kind than those frequently committed by ideologically fanatical radio talk-show hosts.

Aristotle said that achieving the good life was largely a matter of mistake avoidance. The point can be extended to the project of good philosophizing. This chapter is about mistakes to avoid in your own philosophizing. Of course, you should look for these mistakes when critically evaluating the philosophizing of others.

Self-Stultification

You needn't bother with the reasons offered in support of a view if the view suffers from some variety of self-stultification. *Stultus* is the Latin adjective for "foolish," and to hold a self-stultifying view is ultimately to make a fool of oneself, intellectually speaking. A self-stultifying view self-destructs under scrutiny.

There are, however, different kinds of self-stultification. The most obvious way a view can be self-stultifying is for it to be self-contradictory—that is, adherence to the view involves affirming contradictory claims. Perhaps the most famous accusation of such a contradictory stance is already familiar to you: the traditional problem of evil (the *logical* problem of evil) addressed to classical theism. According to classical theists, the world was created by a perfectly good, omnipotent, omniscient being. But classical theists also acknowledge that the world contains much pain and suffering. The objection to theism is then this: these two beliefs are logically contradictory. They are not, note, explicitly contradictory. The idea is that the falsity of the one follows from the supposed truth of the other.

Although this argument seems to be alive and well among educated persons, it's hard to find a philosopher of religion—even a nontheist—anymore who thinks it's a good argument. And it will be instructive to see why, for this will provide you with a general strategy for defending yourself against the objection that two of your beliefs are contradictory. The strategy is known as the Consistency Strategy.

Suppose you believe propositions P and Q, and either you yourself suspect or someone else has suggested that it is impossible for both P and Q to be true. For example, let P be "A person who looks just like Madonna was photographed on Sunset Strip last Saturday," and let Q be "Madonna was in London last Saturday." To show that the suggestion of contradiction is unwarranted, you simply need to find some third proposition R that is possibly true, such that P, Q, and R together form a consistent set of propositions. R needn't be in fact true or known to be true or even plausible. In this case, candidates for R would be "Madonna has a twin sister" and "Madonna has a look-alike." Again, note that, because the charge is that P and Q are logically inconsistent, it doesn't matter whether R is plausible, reasonable, or even likely. R must merely be possibly true and together with P and Q generate a possibly true—that is, consistent—set.

Now you're in a position to see how this applies to the logical problem of evil. But first you'll need one additional ingredient, the idea of a *morally sufficient reason*. A morally sufficient reason is a reason that excuses an agent from blame when that agent has allowed something bad to occur that the agent has the power to prevent. If I have a morally sufficient reason for doing something I had the power not to do, or for allowing something to happen I could have prevented, then, although I am responsible for the situation, I have not acted wrongly. One common sort of morally sufficient reason involves allowing something bad to happen to bring about some greater good, as when the parents of a young child with leukemia allow the child to have an excruciatingly painful bone marrow transplant to save the child's life.

Now consider the following set of statements:

1. God exists.
2. God has a morally sufficient reason for allowing every instance of pain and suffering.
3. There is pain and suffering.

Statement 2 certainly seems to meet the requirements of the Consistency Strategy: it is possibly true. Because 3 actually deductively follows from 1 and 2, it's clear that they tell a logically consistent story. And since 1, 2, and 3 are logically consistent, so must be 1 and 3. By the way, this doesn't mean that there isn't still a powerful argument from the pain and suffering in the world against classical theism. However, because of the success of the Consistency Strategy, the currently popular argument from evil focuses on the plausibility or reasonableness of statement 2, arguing that 2 is possibly true but implausible, given the plenitude of apparently pointless suffering in the world.

The Consistency Strategy is a defensive maneuver. When successful, it shows that the charge of contradictoriness against a view is mistaken. It doesn't, however, provide evidence for the view you use it to defend. That my belief that aliens are secretly visiting my kitchen every night and eating three corn flakes is possibly true is not by itself a reason to believe that it is true. To show that a view is logically consistent merely preserves it as an option on the intellectual playing field.

Another kind of self-stultification occurs when a view by itself provides a conclusive reason for the falsity of the view. Such a view is usually said to be "self-refuting" or "self-defeating," but you may sometimes come across the fancy expression "self-referentially incoherent." In Chapter 4 I argued that this is the problem with the views I called subjectivism and conventionalism. A further and famous example of self-refutation can be found in twentieth-century philosophy. The philosophical movement known as logical positivism was built around the notorious Verification Principle, which says that for a statement to be meaningful (that is, possibly true or false), it must be provable or disprovable by the methods of science or mathematics. The problem is that the principle cannot itself be proved by the methods of science or mathematics. Hence, the principle is meaningless by the standard it itself lays down. Because it undermines the possibility of its own truth, the principle isn't really a viable candidate for belief.

Before proceeding to mistakes in reasoning, I should mention a form of self-stultification that is not strictly the same as the kinds just mentioned. Sometimes philosophers object to a view not because the view itself is self-stultifying but because the *activity* of defending the view undermines the view defended. Let's call this *pragmatic* self-refutation, to distinguish it from the *logical* self-refutation discussed earlier. For example, there is no internal problem with the sentence "I cannot communicate any of my thoughts using the English language." It is even possible to imagine circumstances in which this view would be true—for example, if after a nuclear war I were the only speaker of English remaining in the world. But what I cannot do is communicate my thought to anyone by uttering the sentence, for my intent to communicate makes no sense if my view is correct.

Some contemporary philosophers have objected to *eliminative materialism* on similar grounds. Here, then, is a contemporary example of the accusation of pragmatic self-refutation. According to eliminative materialists, a complete true description of reality will not include such psychological items as beliefs and desires, so a fortiori no rational beliefs. Yet eliminative materialists write books attempting to persuade readers to *believe* that eliminative materialism is true and eminently rational. However, the concept of persuasion seems inextricably tied to the concept of beliefs; if there are no beliefs, there is no persuasion, either. Hence the objection: In the attempt to get other philosophers to change their beliefs, eliminative materialists are doing something that makes sense only if their view is false.

Remember that self-stultification is a strong charge that, if correct, provides the best sort of knock-down objection to a view. But beware of rashness, especially when you realize that you don't really like the view under consideration or that you would prefer that the view is false (as you will almost inevitably realize whenever the truth of the view would imply the falsity of one of your central life-orienting beliefs). Philosophers who hold a controversial view will usually be aware of such objections and provide some response. You should give these responses serious consideration, although you may decide in the end that they are not adequate.

The Epistemic Double Standard

So much for flaws. Now let's begin to look at fallacious reasoning. Self-stultification has to do with the consistency of a view. But consistency also places a constraint on the kinds of reasons we rely on to justify our beliefs, either to ourselves or to others. This brings to mind a fallacy I'm going to call "the fallacy of the epistemic double standard."

Suppose the main case against a defendant in a criminal trial is that several eyewitnesses have identified Mr. Smith as the person they saw driving the getaway car. To undermine this reason for Mr. Smith's complicity, Mr. Smith's attorney calls expert witnesses who testify to the large body of scientific evidence for the general unreliability of eyewitness testimony. The attorney is offering the following argument to the jury: Because eyewitness testimony is generally unreliable, the eyewitness testimony of witnesses who claim to have seen Mr. Smith driving the getaway car is not a good reason to believe Mr. Smith is guilty. Now suppose that, after making this point to the jury, Mr. Smith's attorney calls a witness who testifies that she sold Mr. Smith a hamburger at a hamburger stand across town at the very time that, according to the prosecution, Mr. Smith was seen driving the getaway car away from the bank. The attorney suggests to the jurors that this eyewitness's testimony vindicates Mr. Smith.

What is the problem here? It is this: The defense attorney is trying to use as a good reason for his client's innocence the very same kind of reason that the prosecution has offered as a good reason to support Mr. Smith's guilt. His argument from eyewitness testimony to Mr. Smith's innocence is just like the argument from eyewitness testimony to Mr. Smith's guilt. He is trying to have his evidential cake and eat it too. The two arguments are on a par. Each offers a similar kind of reason in support of a similar kind of conclusion. On pain of inconsistency, having rejected the prosecution's reasoning, Mr. Smith's attorney cannot offer any eyewitness testimony as good evidence for anything.

My favorite example of an epistemic double standard used in philosophizing can unfortunately still be found in numerous introductory philosophy textbooks. The fallacy arises in discussions of the existence of God, and it involves the following assumption: "It is rational to believe that God exists only if there is a valid deductive argument for the existence of God with premises regarded as true *by all sane and reasonable persons.*" A valid argument with such premises would be a deductive proof for its conclusion. A discussion then ensues that shows how no such proof is forthcoming, and the student is encouraged to draw the appropriate conclusion regarding the rationality of theism. By this point you should be able to figure out what is wrong with a philosopher's espousing such a strong epistemic standard. Not only is there no such argument for the philosophical view that God exists but—assuming that philosophers meet the requirement of sanity and reasonableness—there is no such argument for *any* interesting philosophical view. Thus, to allow that theistic belief is irrational because it doesn't meet the standard, but other philosophical beliefs can be *rational* although they too don't meet the standard, is inconsistent in the same way that Mr. Smith's attorney was inconsistent in both accepting and rejecting eyewitness testimony. There may well be reasons that show why belief in God is irrational, but a philosopher who defends its irrationality this way is committing the fallacy of an epistemic double standard.

Circular Arguments

The next fallacy—actually, pair of fallacies—arises when an argument fails to do its job. Consider the following argument:

> Light sometimes behaves like a wave and sometimes like a particle.
> Therefore, light sometimes behaves like a wave and sometimes like a particle.

The premise is true, so the argument is both sound and valid. But something is still wrong with it. It can hardly be taken to establish its conclusion. If you doubted that light sometimes behaves like a wave and sometimes like a particle, this argument would be of little use as a way of showing you that its conclusion is true. Why not? Because the conclusion just is the premise. The argument is *logically circular* or *logically question begging*. An argument is logically circular whenever the conclusion actually figures among the premises.

Philosophers are generally too logically acute to endorse arguments in which the conclusion appears among the premises. When philosophizing, it's more likely that you'll come across arguments that suffer from a more subtle form of circularity—*epistemic* circularity. Consider the following argument:

> Either thoughts are brain states or pigs can fly.
> Pigs can't fly.
> Therefore, thoughts are brain states.

Note that, if thoughts are brain states, this argument is both sound and valid. Moreover, it is not logically circular because the conclusion is not found among the premises. Yet it is circular for the following reason: It is not possible to know or reasonably believe the first premise without relying on the truth of the conclusion. Because it is obvious that pigs can't fly, only someone who already believed the conclusion would accept the first premise.

When you are so captured with the vision of some comprehensive philosophical outlook, it is easy to slip into epistemically circular reasoning unawares. So be careful.

In the last chapter we looked at five different sources of basic beliefs—beliefs that are prima facie rational to hold without basing them on other beliefs. Interestingly, it may well be impossible to offer any argument for the general reliability of a basic belief source that is not epistemically question begging. This point is perhaps most obvious in the case of the reliability of memory. As an exercise, you might try constructing a sound argument that is not epistemically circular for the conclusion "Memory is a reliable source of information about the past." Notice that, to avoid epistemic circularity, the reliability of memory cannot enter into the justification you have for thinking that any of the premises are true.

False Generalization and False Dilemma

One of the first things you must do when thinking about a philosophical question is to decide on the available answers worthy of consideration. For this reason, it is especially important that you characterize a position accurately. The danger of wrongly characterizing is strongest when you are asking questions that involve some widely recognized "ism," questions such as "Is dualism true?" "Does naturalism provide an accurate account of such and such?" "Is theism true?" "Is determinism compatible with free will?" and so on. The problem is that each of these "isms" denotes not a single philosophical view but a family of views that share some core claims in common. Some mind-body dualists don't believe in the existence of

a human soul; others do. Some theists think God has per-
fect foreknowledge of all future events; others don't. A
good argument against one variety of dualism or theism
or naturalism may not be a good argument against some
other variety. Of course, it is philosophical progress for
you personally if you find yourself to have discovered a
good argument against one clearly defined view. But
don't make a mistake like the man who asked whether
animals could fly and decided they can't because the only
animal he considered was a cow.

I don't think there is a recognized name for the mistake in philosophizing I'm warning you against here. Let's
just call it the fallacy of *false philosophical generalization—
false generalization* for short. When you find the fallacy of
false generalization in a philosopher's line of reasoning,
another fallacy is usually lurking in the wings—namely,
the fallacy of *false dilemma.* The rhetorical game works as
follows. After asking a philosophical question such as
"What is the nature of the relation between the human
mind and the human body?" a philosopher says that one
of either two views must be correct—in this case, say, dualism or materialism. Dualism is then defined as, say,
Descartes's dualism, which is then, according to the
writer, easily shown to be silly and implausible. This leaves
materialism as the only intellectual option left standing.
The problem is that we have been given no reason to
think that Descartes's variety of dualism should be considered the most viable candidate for consideration or, for
that matter, that the version of materialism proposed is
itself the best going version. There are, indeed, non-
Cartesian dualists, and sometimes a dualist such as
Thomas Aquinas seems to be saying very much what some
contemporary materialists say. Some contemporary dualists share with Descartes the rejection of materialism, but
they deny that human beings have a supernatural soul, as
Descartes believed. The benefit of a false dilemma to a
philosopher who employs it is that it is quick and easy.
The problem with a false dilemma is that it is too quick
and easy.

Philosophizing Belief Policies

This completes the list of flaws and fallacies that, in addition to the mistakes canvassed in our discussion of deductive, inductive, and best-explanation arguments, you are most likely to encounter when philosophizing. Together they provide you with a set of belief policies to follow when you think philosophically:

1. Avoid self-stultifying views.
2. Don't use an epistemic double standard in evaluating philosophical claims.
3. Avoid logically circular arguments.
4. Avoid epistemically circular arguments.
5. Always clearly and carefully define a philosophical view under consideration.
6. Don't commit the fallacy of false philosophical generalization.
7. Avoid false dilemmas.

As I said at the beginning of this chapter, good philosophizing is partly a matter of mistake avoidance. Follow these belief policies, and you'll have a good start at becoming a skilled philosophical reasoner and critic.

CHAPTER 11

Reasons, Judgment, and Trust

ONE SUMMER EVENING YEARS AGO IN WISCONSIN, AS I STOOD OUT-side on the lawn with a friend, I remarked on the surprising number of bats feeding in the clear, darkening sky. He replied that he was certain I was mistaken: what looked like bats to me were in fact swallows. I was certain (and indeed still am certain) that it was he, not I, who erred. Yet as we stood there looking at the relevant evidence, there was no way for me to *show* him that his perceptual judgment was mistaken. Furthermore, I could hardly fault him for holding his belief, and I surely would not have accused him of irrationality. He was basing his perceptual belief on the right sort of evidence, and I could even understand how someone might mistake these swift little bats for swallows. From my perspective, the disagreement arose because of some defect in his epistemic position, a defect that rendered him insensitive to the subtle indicators of bats and swallows. In other words, I didn't think that he had the capacity to distinguish rapidly flying bats from rapidly flying swallows at dusk. He was properly basing his judgment of what he "saw"; he just wasn't seeing the right things. By rejecting his belief, and thereby sustaining our disagreement, I was implicitly committing myself to the superiority of my epistemic position over his. By trusting what my visual experience "told" me, I was rejecting what his "told" him. However—and this is the interesting point—I could not defend the superiority of my epistemic position in a non-question-begging fashion. For to say that his epistemic position, unlike mine, is defective, is just to say that he, unlike me, does not perceptually judge things as they really are. And "how things really are" is what is at issue.

Having and Giving Reasons

We often assume that reasons are like apples—the sort of thing that if I indeed *have* one, I can easily *give* it to someone else. According to this assumption, if I have a reason to believe proposition P, then I should be able to give you or anyone else *my* reason for believing thus. And just as you can scrutinize the apple I give you to see whether it is rotten or tasty, so you can evaluate the reason to see whether it is a bad or good one. The assumption works well so long as my reason for believing that P is an argument with other beliefs of mine for premises and P for the conclusion. Because arguments are propositional in nature, I can give you my reason in this case by telling you my argument through writing or speaking. When my belief is based on other stateable beliefs of mine, the evidence I possess is *propositional evidence,* and I may express my reason for belief in the form of an argument.

With an argument, you can lay all of your evidential cards on the table.

However, although arguments are useful tools for showing someone else why you hold a particular belief, there are limits on the role arguments can play as evidence. As we have already seen, many beliefs simply arise in us as the (fallible) deliverances of perception, memory, sensation, reason, and testimony. As I stood looking at the bats at dusk, my belief was not directly based on or generated by other stateable beliefs of mine but based on my *experience* of seeing the flying creatures. They looked like bats to me, and if my friend Fred had demanded a justification for my view, I would probably have said, "Well, I can see that they are bats and not swallows. Swallows don't look like that in flight." My visual experience in the story is a piece of *nonpropositional evidence* for my belief. And, because no one but me can have my experiences, I can hardly give this evidence to Fred or anyone else.

I could, of course, present Fred with the following argument as we gaze skyward in disagreement:

1. These flying creatures look like bats in flight.
2. If these flying creatures look like bats in flight, then they are bats.

Therefore, these flying creatures are bats.

However, although I will think this argument sound if it occurs to me, it is not my reason for believing its conclusion. And Fred doesn't accept premise 1 anyway. His visual experience is "telling" him that the only bats are in my mental belfry. So long as neither of us has any reason to doubt the reliability of what our respective visual experiences seem to indicate, our little dispute is unlikely to be resolved.

Consider a second scenario. Suppose my friends and I know that I have a habit of procrastination, that in the past I have failed on several occasions to mail in my tax return on time, and that the IRS has informed me that, yet again this year, my tax return was filed late. With these propositions as premises, my friends and I have available a strong argument for the conclusion that I probably filed late this year. However, suppose I remember mailing my return a week before the deadline. My memory provides me with nonpropositional evidence unavailable to my friends. In that case, it would be perfectly rational for me to believe myself guiltless, while it would not be irrational for my friends to believe me at fault.

These stories illustrate a useful epistemological distinction between *being justified in holding a belief* and *showing that one is justified in holding a belief.* Being justified is a state or condition, while showing that one is justified is a process. The bat and tax return cases illustrate that I may be justified in holding a belief even though it is impossible for me to show that I am justified. Indeed, because it is impossible for me to give Fred and my friends my reasons for belief directly (in the way I could give you an argument), I may be unable to persuade them in each case that it is they who are mistaken, not I. But the key point is that I cannot impugn either Fred or my friends for being irrational.

Philosophizing and Rational Judgment

What does all of this have to do with philosophizing? Quite a lot, actually. Because philosophizing is essentially conversational, philosophers have understandably tended to focus on communicable reasons (that is, arguments) as the means of justifying beliefs. However, the defense of any well-articulated philosophical position inevitably involves controversial premises that do not command the assent of all rational persons. A *compelling* argument would be an argument all of whose premises (as well as any assumptions required to accept the argument as a good reason in support of its conclusion) have the following feature: it could not be rejected by any honest, serious, logically acute philosopher who understood it and reflected on its truth. Historically, philosophers who wish to defend perennially disputed philosophical views have had dubious success in finding such arguments. (After all, if such arguments were at hand, then most philosophical disputes would have been resolved—or at least taken to be resolved—by all serious inquirers everywhere.)

Consider a common enough story. Suppose that Professors Jones and Davis are highly distinguished, world-famous philosophers by the sort of standards that establish such pedigree. Each has published numerous highly acclaimed books and articles. They are old friends, having studied together as doctoral students at Oxford University. Jones has taught for over thirty years at Cornell, during which time Davis has been a member of the Oxford faculty. Each has a long-standing interest in the question "What is the relation between the mental and the physical?" Jones has written extensively in defense of a reductionistic account of the mental, according to which mental phenomena are taken to be identical to physical phenomena. Davis thinks (and has always thought) that Jones's view is utterly implausible and has written extensively in defense of the view that the mental is something distinct from though causally related to the physical. Each of them has studied and fully understands the other's arguments, yet each remains convinced that the other is mistaken.

What I want to suggest is that the dispute between Jones and Davis is in an interesting way similar to my dispute with Fred over bats and swallows. The key difference is that what may be called "rational judgment" plays the role in the philosophical dispute played by perceptual judgment in my dispute over the bats with Fred. One can even imagine Jones saying to Davis, "I understand your argument. I just don't see that the conclusion follows. And I can't make any sense of the second premise. I don't at all see why it *has* to be true. Indeed, it seems to me obviously false." Although Davis can give Jones her arguments, she cannot give Jones her rational assessment of those arguments. Whether these rational assessments simply happen to one (like a pain) or are something one does (like trying to catch a ball), they are nontransferably one's own.

Rational judgment plays an uneliminable role in philosophizing in at least two places. First, a philosopher must rely on her rational judgment to provide her with unargued-for premises she takes for granted and that seem to her immune to refutation. A philosopher will typically be just as certain that she "sees" the truth of such premises as I am certain that I saw bats, not swallows, in flight. The tacit appeal to self-evidence or rational intuition, to what "just makes sense" (or not) to the inquirer, plays an extraordinarily important role in reasoning about controversial philosophical matters. Second, a philosopher must rely on his rational judgment when deliberating about whether a conclusion or premise really is supported by the arguments and evidence adduced in its favor. If the relevant arguments and evidence are sufficiently complex and the concepts employed sufficiently difficult to grasp and wield, it is very likely that reasonable philosophers will disagree about the correct assessment of the arguments and evidence.

Understanding Philosophical Disagreements

Here I should add several caveats. The fact that in our philosophizing we, like Jones and Davis, may not be able to see our way to a consensus on the truth does not mean that there is no truth to the matter (this was one of the main points of Chapter 4). Moreover, it would be a mistake to think that because philosophers disagree about *some* philosophical matters they disagree about *everything*. Jones and Davis, for example, will share an educated, critical, reflective understanding of subtle, highly technical conceptual distinctions relevant to their dispute. They will be acquainted with historically important (and often difficult) arguments and theories in the philosophy of mind. There is no easy and quick route to such understanding, which can only be gained through hours, weeks, and even years of study and reflection. They will know the standard objections to their respective positions. They will both be familiar with the demonstrably bad arguments that have been offered for their views and be able to explain what's wrong with those arguments. They will probably agree on many points about the strengths and weaknesses of their views. Furthermore, in other philosophical arenas independent of their dispute in the philosophy of mind—for example, in ethics or the philosophy of science—they may wholeheartedly agree.

I am also not suggesting that the final arbiter in all or even most philosophical disputes is mere personal taste and sentiment. Jones's and Davis's philosophical disagreements are not just like their disagreements about, say, whether broccoli tastes good or jazz music is pleasant to the ear. That personal judgment plays an ineradicable role in philosophizing does not mean that everyone's philosophical beliefs are held in the same way. All of us have interesting philosophical beliefs. But not all of us have endeavored to philosophize about those beliefs, to subject them to critical scrutiny, to evaluate the arguments and evidence for and against them.

Thinking about philosophical questions is often difficult and tedious, but it is something at which, like playing the piano or reading topographical maps, you can get better with time and practice. There are certainly persons who agree with Jones's view of mental phenomena but have never philosophized about it. The difference between that person's belief and Jones's belief is that Jones has subjected his belief to long-term scrutiny and reflection, in light of what others have said on the topic, and he is prepared and able to give a defense of his position.

To philosophize well you must develop specialized intellectual habits and skills relevant to understanding and evaluating philosophical views. With effort, you can get better at such things as recognizing faulty reasoning, spotting confused thinking, and teasing out hidden assumptions from a complex argument. It stands to reason that beginners at philosophizing will not be as good as experienced practitioners. Moreover, those better at philosophizing will be more strongly warranted in trusting their judgments when philosophizing.

Perhaps an analogy will help out here. Suppose I find myself with a complex and rare set of symptoms that could be caused by one of several rare tropical diseases. Whose diagnosis is more likely to be correct, that of a student in her second year of medical school or that of a physician who has specialized in the diagnosis and treatment of rare tropical diseases for the past thirty years? Clearly, the latter. Yet we can easily imagine that two equally specialized and experienced physicians may disagree on the correct diagnosis in a difficult case, the one judging that disease X is the cause of the symptoms, the other judging that disease Y is the cause. They can't both be correct, but their educated opinions, informed by long experience, should be taken seriously.

Why Philosophizing Can't Be a Spectator Sport

You should be aware of two rhetorical devices contemporary philosophers use to mask over the role of personal judgment in philosophizing. The first trick is to employ the first-person plural pronoun *we* when presenting controversial claims. For example: "We would hoot anyone off the podium if they suggested that it is impossible to build a computer that can think." The reader is left with the impression that (1) she, the reader, is a member of an enlightened coterie of informed, reasonable persons and (2) anyone who disagrees with "what we think" is ignorant, irrational, or worse. Of course, this is just an obvious instance of question-begging rhetoric.

The second trick, which often is found in tandem with the use of *we*, is to appeal to the majority opinion of professional philosophers. There is an ironic twist when a philosopher makes it clear that he regards this a reason to adopt his view. Good philosophers tend to pride themselves on their ability to "think for themselves." Yet appeal to majority opinion is just a crass appeal to authority, which amounts to the recommendation "Trust the judgment of the majority." This advice is unflatteringly close to "Don't think for yourself. Leave the serious thinking to us majority-view philosophers." Anyway, given what you know about the diversity of views in the history of philosophy and about the very nature of philosophizing, you probably realize that the appeal to majority opinion doesn't count for much. If one person's reasoning can be defective, so can the reasoning of lots of persons.

Suppose you want to jump into the philosophical fray and decide for yourself whether Professor Jones or Professor Davis is correct about the nature of the relation between the mental and the physical. In that case, you have no choice but to do as Jones and Davis must do. You must trust in the general reliability of your own intellectual capacities and rational judgments to produce an answer that is true or likely true. You must trust that a sort of personal, intellectual experience familiar to philosophers will be truth-conducive—that the experience, in this case, of inquiring into the evidence and arguments for and against Jones's and Davis's respective positions will result in true or likely true beliefs about the correctness of their views. If you are going to philosophize, you have no option but to do so.

Suppose that you decide, after long and careful study of the arguments of Jones and Davis, that you agree with Davis, not Jones. Then you, like Davis, will find yourself committed to a view of Jones's rational judgment vis-à-vis the arguments that is analogous to my view of Fred's perceptual judgment vis-à-vis the bats. You will be committed to the view that there is some defect in Jones's intellectual makeup that prevents him from being able to correctly evaluate the evidence available to him. Like Davis, by rejecting Jones's arguments and conclusion, you are implicitly committing yourself to the superiority of your (and Davis's) epistemic position over Jones's. By trusting what your rational judgment "tells" you, you are thereby rejecting what Jones's rational judgment "tells" him. Still, you can hardly fault Jones for trusting his rational judgment, since you would never have arrived at your position had you not trusted your own judgment. Moreover, without begging the question, you will not be able to show that Jones's condition is defective. For in this context to say that his epistemic condition is defective is to say that Jones, unlike Davis and yourself, does not rationally assess things to be as they really are. And "how things really are" is what is at issue.

Philosophizing, like all other intellectual investigation into issues about which the "experts" disagree, requires in the long run a healthy degree of intellectual confidence in oneself and one's ability to get at the truth. There is no non-question-begging *guarantee* that by trusting your rational judgment in the course of philosophizing or by relying on your assessment of the evidence you will arrive at true or likely true beliefs. The risk of error is ineradicable. We are all of us working without a net.

Yet trust you must, if you choose to philosophize. If you choose not to philosophize, you can hardly argue for the reasonableness of your choice.

I N D E X

agreement-fact, 52–53
Aquinas, Thomas, 116
argument from design, 84–85
arguments, 79
   to best explanation, 91
   compelling,122
   deductive, 80, 85–88
   inductive, 83, 88–91
   reductio ad absurdum, 82

belief, 29–32
   basic, 98
   and caring about truth, 57–65
   degrees of, 40
   and explaining action, 60
   life-orienting, 61
   management of, 67–79
   reporting and endorsing, 32
   sources of, 97
belief policies, 68
   and arguments, 85–90
   need for, 67–71
   for philosophizing, 117
   selecting, 76
   and subjective rationality, 73
Buddhism, 93

classical theism, 63, 65, 93, 108
conceptual distinctions, 51
Consistency Strategy, 109
concepts, 43
conventionalism, 38–39, 110
Corbett, Jim, 104
correctness, 8
   of belief policies, 73
   of beliefs, 54
   of philosophizing, 124–126
   two kinds of, 12–13

counterexamples, 48

determinism, 87, 115
Descartes, 76, 116
dualism, 115–116

Einstein, 25, 102
eliminative materialism, 111
epistemic double standard, 112–
   113
epistemic circularity, 114–115

facts, 52–54
faith, 104
false dilemma, 116
false philosophical generalization,
   115–116
free will, 12, 18, 26, 87

God, 6, 12, 26, 33, 44, 62–63, 113,
   116
Gould, Stephen Jay, 90

happiness, 59

introspection, 100
intuitions, 51,124

James, William, 90

knowledge, 4
   as justified true belief, 50–52

logical circularity, 114
logical inconsistency, 86–87
logical problem of evil, 108–110

metaphysics, 5

memory, 97
morally sufficient reason, 109

necessary conditions, 46–47
Newton, 101
nonpropositional evidence, 121–
122

objective fact, 53–54
objective reality, 33–34

Peirce, C. S., 91
perception, 99
philosophical behaviorism, 18, 49–
50
philosophical definitions, 49
philosophical naturalism, 63, 65,
93, 115
philosophical questions, 15–20, 23
philosophizing, 1
central subactivities of, 7–9
mistakes in, 107
not set of doctrines, 11
obstacles to, 10–11
and rational judgment, 123–128
and trust, 127–128
and worldviews, 64
propositional evidence, 121–122

rationality, 71
objective, 74
subjective, 72

rational judgment, 123–128
rattlesnakes, 59
reason, 100
reasons, having and giving, 120

science, 13, 17, 24, 77, 90, 103
scientism, 84
self-contradiction, 108
self-evident truths, 101
self-refutation, 110–111
logical, 110
pragmatic, 111
Skinner, B. F., 18
sources of belief, 97
subjectivism, 36–39, 110
sufficient and necessary conditions,
47–48
sufficient conditions, 45–46

telepathy, 104
testimony, 102–104
time machine, 82
"true for me," 35
truth, 34

Verification Principle, 110

worldviews, 63–64
and philosophizing, 64, 93–94